AN ATTEMPT TO REPAIR AMERICA'S BROKEN CREDIT SYSTEM

The Legal Loopholes The Credit Bureaus Don't Want You To Know

By

Andre' Coakley

Published by Andre Coakley www.andrecoakley.com

Publisher's Cataloging-in-Publication data Andre Coakley

An Attempt to Repair America's Broken Credit System

The Legal Loopholes The Credit Bureaus Don't Want You To Know

Andre Coakley — 1st ed. p. cm.

Printed in the United States of America. First Edition

TABLE OF CONTENTS

Introduction

When it comes to repairing your credit, you have to be smart about it. Granted, there are hundreds of infomercials out there conning people out of their hard-earned cash with empty promises. This book is nothing like that—its only goal is to serve you the nitty-gritty of how to raise your credit score while beating the system legally.

The American credit system is a dangerous game for serious players only. This guide offers you the known and hidden rules of the games so you will not have to waste money on debt counseling organizations or some online credit repair sales trick.

All you have is to take a trip into the underworld of the American credit system and win this game legally. In this book, you will see copies of creditor correspondence, real-life story examples, time-tested techniques to raise your score and much more.

One sweet thing about being American is that you cannot be imprisoned for being broke—tax evasion and fraud may get you behind bars, but never for being in debt. Of course, when done right, you can use debt to your advantage (a knowledge very few are privy of), accumulating wealth in the process. The key is owning your credit score.

Unfortunately, compulsive spending has been ingrained in consumers nowadays. Conspicuous ads are always trying to manipulate you into purchasing something beyond your means. Of course, there is always a creditor at hand to smoothen the process of wrecking your finances.

While this guide is not about compulsive spending, it will teach you how to get a higher credit score, enjoy lower interest rates and be rewarded with improved financing terms by playing the credit game well.

Get a highlighter and give this guide your undivided attention. You are about to catch the secrets your creditors, and reporting agencies are keeping from you.

CHAPTER 1

The Agencies and the Laws of Credit Reporting

This Chapter Lectures About:

- Who are the CRA's? - Credit Reporting Agencies
- Understanding the FCRA – Fair Credit Reporting Act
- Breaking Down The FACT Act – The Fair and Accurate Credit Transactions

Know this—America is thriving with millions of people in debt. Your case is nothing special. Just on credit cards alone, most people have maxed over $10,000. The problem is, a large percentage of them have ruined their credit score at some point, incurring the wrath of higher interest rates, fees, and penalties on these monies borrowed.

If your credit score is in the 600's or lower, it's time for you to remove the stress by understanding the rules of the game. It is never too late to improve your credit rating. Whether you are fresh to the game or have been stuck with a poor credit score for a long time, past errors can still be repaired—a more prosperous and brighter future is always possible.

This book aims to give you the highest score possible by preparing you for the moments when you have to use your credit score to get a credit card, a car, a house or even a job.

Credit Reporting Agencies

Creditors are institutions who lend you money in the form of loans and credit cards who have a level of measuring trust called "creditworthiness." This helps them in determining whether you will pay before the due date. Also, when you do not pay up, they also have a disciplinary method to apply.

This is where selling credit reports or "report cards" on consumers come in. During the credit boom and the rise of new-age computer technology in the 1960s, thousands of lending companies (local and international) and credit reporting agencies blossomed. Today, after decades of buyouts and mergers, we now have three major credit reporting agencies responsible for compiling your reports.

They include Equifax, Experian (known formerly as TRW), and TransUnion.

By definition, credit reporting agencies are profit-driven organizations responsible for gathering and selling consumer information—particularly the financial history of consumers. In the beginning, these companies tagged themselves as "bureaus" and "agencies"—thus fostering their plan to self-promote themselves to carry on a common but baseless public opinion that these companies are associated with the federal government. In reality, they have no link with the government. They are just private organizations; because of that, they have loosely branded themselves as credit reporting "agencies," aka CRAs.

Historically, CRAs would supply information to just about anybody seeking information and with cash to pay. Back in the day, technology was not, of course, like it is in our present time. Therefore, CRAs have taken on this notorious reputation for their little or no concern for completeness or accuracy of with data files of thousands of consumers. Still, they are growing at a break-neck speed. These companies made dreadful errors over the years—and lucky for them, the majority of the 50 state lawmakers could be less concerned until recently. Thankfully, the federal government stepped in—drafted new laws and legislated CRAs' requirements—to amend a boatload of issues.

The Fair Credit Reporting Act (FCRA)

In 1971, Congress finally enacted the Fair Credit Reporting Act (FCRA). The basic premise of this Act can be broken into two primary goals:

1. Enabling consumers to get reports of their personal financial history from CRAs by just asking for it.

2. Requiring both the CRAs and their suppliers of information to obey specific regulations and procedures on the maintenance of consumer information.

By the way, the FCRA only covers consumer credit transactions. It does not apply to commercial credit transactions like huge insurance transactions and specific business loan—commercial reporting agencies handle these; Dun & Bradstreet is one well-known example.

Provided below is a direct excerpt from the Federal Trade Commission aptly named "FCRA Summary of Rights." It is worth the read because this document will keep popping up when you are applying for credit and mortgages.

FCRA Summary of Rights

Apart from granting you specific rights, the FCRA also grants the CRAs some rights too. For instance, they are permitted to show your report to anybody with a business need that is genuine. This list does not just cover your prospective and current creditors (e.g., credit card companies, banks and mortgage lenders); it can also include insurance companies, employers and even landlords. Worryingly, CRAs has the right to market the accessibility of your credit file to people you do not know (especially solicitors who can get your credit report anytime and without your knowledge or permission). Now you know the source of all that junk mail.

TIP: To end those unwanted financial offers (e.g., insurance products and credits) from being mailed to you, you can decide on looking on the solicitation's toll-free number (legally required)—or you can opt for the more preventive option of barring these strangers entirely by:

- Calling the toll-free number servicing all three credit reporting agencies: (888) 567-8688.
- Visit www.OptOutPrescreen.com and select from one of two options: i) Opt out temporarily for the next five years via the website or ii) permanently by via a mail-in form.

Nowadays, the CRAs can get away with reporting the wrong information as long as they follow specific guidelines. Another disturbing thing is, they are not legally obligated to notify you when unfavorable information is being reported about you. Moreover, they are now monetizing the notification of negative information to consumers by marketing monitoring services to them. Think about it. This means you have to pay to catch a wrong reporting error about your financial information.

Wrapping up, seeing your report is your legal right—many other strangers have that right as well. Keep in mind CRAs are not held accountable for the correctness of the information in your file and are not obligated to notify when unfavorable information is being reported about you. This explains why a truckload of errors keeps hurting the credit files of thousands of consumers annually.

The Fair and Accurate Credit Transactions Act (FACT Act)

Apart from the real errors that may show in your credit file, thousands of consumers are suffering from deliberate errors called identity theft. Between April 2016 and April 2017, 18.4 million cases of identity theft were reported by consumers with losses grossing up to $16 billion (U.S. Federal Trade Commission report, 2016).

Three goals of the FACT Act:

1. Ensuring that lenders make loan decisions founded on comprehensive and open credit histories, instead of discriminatory stereotypes.
2. Protecting consumers against identity theft by improving the credit information quality
3. Giving consumers the right to request a copy of their credit report once a year that's free of charge.

The FACT Act clears up much legal mumbo-jumbo of state regulations and laws concerning how consumers should and must report identity theft and how credit card companies, reporting agencies and banks must respond.

In Chapter 4, you will learn to get a free copy of your credit report once a year.

In Chapter 15, you will be provided with two methods of safeguarding yourself from identify theft.

CHAPTER 2

Working with the Data

This Chapter Lectures About:

- Who Collects Credit Reporting Data?
- Why Should You Care About Your Credit Score?

If the microchip in the computer was not invented, the three-digit number you know as a credit score would never exist. Your credit score is based on convoluted mathematical algorithms so intricate a statistician would spend several hours calculating it to get a final number. These calculations depend on large amounts of data that are stored for over a decade. If not for the computer, many would get away getting their dream car or home, instead of working for a good score—a score that is controlled by updated data every month.

The fact is, every single thing you do, gets an update to your credit file. At any point in time, your data can be collected and calculated for risk.

It starts with your first engagement with a creditor during a consumer to business financial transaction—the data collection is continuous and only ends until you have fulfilled the terms of your agreement. However, everything stays put on your report for another seven years.

All through the length of this relationship, the creditor gathers information and reports it to the CRA; this information may include your payment history, phone number, and home address, and much more. If you think you are safe because you did not submit your social security number (SSN) or provided a fake one, think again. By just using your home address and name, a creditor is capable of effortlessly reporting your information. This is how several bad checks, public record and collection accounts keep appearing on your credit reports.

Who's Responsible for Reporting Information to the CRAs:

The sample list below shows the standard type of businesses that can report information about you.

Credit Card Companies:
Apart from significant credit card companies, department stores, and gasoline companies can also report your credit history.

Banks and Lenders:
These include the offerings of a bank or lender—from lines of credit to mortgages to auto loans.

Student Loans:
Student loan (private and federal) payment history and failures.

Collection Agencies:
These are private companies that report on defaulted accounts bought by them or allocated to them. Defaulted accounts may include medical bills, utilities, credit cards, and loans.

Local, State and Federal Governments:
This can range from bankruptcy filings to child support to tax liens.

Insurance Agencies:
Insurance agencies can report information on your insurance application—along with deficient balances owed to the insurance agency due to underpaid premiums or overpaid proceeds, plus your obligations to third-party insurance agencies in case of self-caused damage while non-insured or under-insured.

Landlords:
Most landlords may not bother to report if your payment history is good. However, they will report an eviction, judgment or collection when their rent is not paid or when their property is damaged.

Utility Companies:
Lately, some utility companies have begun to report payment histories; however, the significant remarks shown on your credit file will likely be as a result of a bill you did miss several months ago.

As it would be expanded upon in this guide, you know that there is a difference between a creditor and a collector.

The FCRA defines a creditor as anyone who is offering or extending credit thus creating a debt or someone who is in debt. On the other hand, collectors are parties that accept the transfer of a debt in a default stage (or an assignment) with the sole aim of collecting debt for another party.

Watch out:
every financial move you make—even with the omission of your social security number—can be reported to the CRAs. We live in a world of information and personal data; every transaction you make requires some verification that includes private information such as date of birth, address and social security number. Even with just your social security number, your phone number and address can be easily retrieved.

What Is a Credit Score and Why Should You Care About It?

A credit score is a convoluted mathematical algorithm that is highly exclusive, and it is used in calculating your financial risk levels from a range of 350 to 850.

So, for a creditor to determine whether you are worth doing business with, a bunch of complex high school like arithmetic equations are needed.

The most well-known credit score is the FICO score (named after its creator, the Fair Isaac Company). The primary use of a FICO score is for predicting your probable rate of delinquency over the next two years. Simply put, they want to know, what are the chances that you are going to fall behind on payments? This score serves as a tool for assessing the risk of doing business with you; it is also the premise of setting the terms of your down payment and interest rate.

Now, what are those major factors affecting the complex mathematical algorithm that determines your credit score?

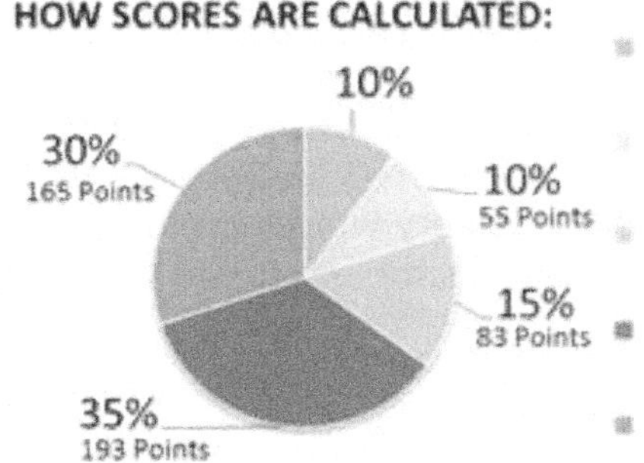

35% - PAYMENT HISTORY = 192.5 Points

30% - UTILIZATION RATIO = 165 Points

15% - LENGTH OF CREDIT HISTORY = 82.5 Points

10% - TYPES OF CREDIT = 55 Points

10% - CREDIT INQUIRIES = 55 Points

The Five Major Factors Making up Your Credit Score:

Today we will be giving you the road map to what makes up a perfect 850 credit score. We want to let you know that credit scores are broken up into five categories. Your score ranges from 300 to 850 on the widely used FICO scoring model. This means you have 550 points to play with, so let us break down those five parts and explain how to maximize that 550 point margin.

1. Payment History - 35% or 192.5 Credit Points

The first part of your score is your payment history which accounts for 35 percent of your credit score or 192.5 points. Factors such as paying your bills on time, collections and charge-off's also count towards your payment history. The first thing any lender wants to know is the timeliness of your past and current payment history. This is one of the most critical factors in building a healthy credit score. A few late payments are not automatic "score-killers." Overall a good payment history can outweigh one or two late payments. However, having no late payments on your credit report does not mean you will get a "perfect score" either. Your payment history is just one of the categories used in calculating your credit scores.

The explanation is quite simple. Late payments cause the most significant damage to your credit score. This covers collection accounts (a past-due account sold or assigned to a collection company for further collection attempts) and charged-off accounts (also a past-due account that has been given up for lost on the tax return of the creditor on the notion that the account will stay unpaid). However, when payments are made consistently and on time, especially for 12 months, your credit score will improve. If you pay all of your bills on time and do not get any collections or charge-off's you should maximize all 192.5 points in this category.

2. Utilization Ratios - 30% or 165 Credit Points

The next category is your credit utilization ratio which accounts for 30 percent of your credit score or 165 points. Therefore, it is essential that you have a revolving account which is a credit card or a store card, but make sure the balance you carry on is very low. Most people will recommend at least 30 percent or lower. However, we recommend a balance of less than 7% percent on credit cards. We have seen credit scores go from an 800 credit score to below the 700's by merely maxing out credit cards. If you are not paying your credit cards on time or are maxing them out, you can lose up to 165 points, if you're not careful. We always recommend getting credit cards, but we also recommend being responsible for them. That is why it is always good to have at least two to three open credit cards minimum. Keeping the utilization ratio low on each card will help to ensure you use credit for emergency purposes only. Practicing this habit daily will make you more responsible for your credit. Remember, banks love lending money to responsible borrowers!

The outstanding balances on your revolving accounts (e.g., credit cards, department store cards, and gasoline cards) are leading factors that affect your report. According to the FICO model, not paying off your balance every month shows your poor money managing skills. Even if your credit file remains unchanged and the single varying factor is your increasing credit card balance, your credit will decrease.

Let's say at the end of month, you have some extra cash and you want to add a little extra to your bills. Rather than trying to spread your payments to all your credit cards, why not put the chunk of your spare cash toward clearing smaller balances first—your aim here is to zero them out very quickly. Doing this will significantly increase your score because even a balance of one dollar still indicates an unpaid balance in the eyes of FICO.

Now, you can move on to the next smallest balance, taking a bottom to top approach, until all your balances are cleared. However, this method goes against the mathematical principle of taking out high-interest-rate accounts first. But if your goal is to improve your bottom-line score the zeroing-out technique is best.

Note: Installment balances (e.g., personal loans, boat loans, auto loans) can affect your credit score, but its effect is not as high as the number of revolving balances to their credit limits. Take for instance a credit card with a $10,000 limit and a $7,000 balance has more of a negative impact than a car loan that began with a $10,000 balance and has since been paid down to a $7,000 balance.

3. Length of Credit History - 15% or 82.5 Credit Points

The length of credit history is depended upon your oldest account, how long you have been using credit and the average age of accounts that you have open right now. This section makes up 15 percent of your score or 82.5 points. So, you want to be very careful with opening credit cards and closing them once the balance is paid off. If you do have credit cards and you are responsible with them, once you pay the balances off, you do not want to close those account unless the cost of annual fees is more of a burden than keeping that credit card open. However, let us say, you opened and maintained your first credit card in college which will help your length of credit history because banks and lenders will look at you as a more responsible borrower. If you can have credit cards open for ten years or longer, you will be seen as more trustworthy. This is precisely the reason why when you pay your mortgage or car loans off early, it is excellent for your payment history, but it could cause a ding in the average age category. So, make sure you that you take care of those older accounts. They are more valuable than you may think!

The longer you are associated as a customer to a particular creditor, the better for you. New accounts are particularly considered risky which makes the computer algorithms automatically identify you as low risk because of your longer account history.

4. New Credit Inquires - 10% or 55 Credit Points

Now let us look at the next category, Credit Inquiries, which accounts for 10 percent or 55 points of your overall score. You do not want to keep applying for new credit because banks look at that as a risk. If you open or apply for a credit card today at Wells Fargo, even with an 800 score, it may be harder to get one tomorrow at Bank of America because of the Wells Fargo credit inquiry. This is why banks usually want to wait 60 days to 90 days before giving you new credit after recent inquiries. They are skeptical and not sure if the prior lenders gave you credit just days before. This is the reason why you want to make sure you never apply for things unless you need, other than a credit card. However, if you do have a credit card, it is a lot easier to ask for a credit limit increase with a good score than to keep doing damage by applying for a new one. Every hard inquiry you have is responsible for taking points off your credit score which could potentially lead up to losing all 55 points. So, you want to make sure you are not applying for new credit regularly.

It is true: new inquiries and new accounts coming from credit applications can lower your score. Opening new accounts may hurt your score for about six months plus you may also see a drop of up to 5 points for every inquiry you make when applying for credit.

5. Types of Credit - 10% or 55 Credit Points

The last category is types of credit which accounts for 10 percent or 55 points of your credit score. This is where we like to explain that you want to make sure you have at least three open credit cards and two installment loans open. Credit cards and lines of credit are the two most common forms of revolving credit. With revolving credit, your credit limit does not change when you make payments on your credit account. You can return to your account to borrow additional money as often as you want, as long as you do not exceed your maximum limits. However, installment credit is paid back with scheduled, periodic payments, involving the gradual reduction of principal and eventual full repayment, ending the credit cycle. Some of you may have open student loans, or you may have them paid off which are still counted as installment loans. Accounts such as car notes and personal loans also fall under the installment loan category. The utilization category is not affected by installment loans, but it can begin to establish a good payment history. If you have installment loans, revolving accounts, open-end accounts, and mortgage accounts, you can maximize the full 10% in this category which is approximately 55 points.

Amazingly, your score is not impacted by the type of accounts you keep. However, having several many revolving accounts affects your score less than even having an equal number of installment loans. While the formula FICO seems to be top-secret, there is intense speculation that mortgages are rated higher than the more rigid finance companies and revolving account—subject to the number of accounts and their maintenance.

Moving away from the primary factors making up your score, you have to know the meaning of your score. The FICO score, ranging from 350 to 850, works on the premise of the "higher, the score better." It is used to assess the chance of you making good on your commitment on a current or new credit obligation over the next two years to come. A historical comparison of your score is made with other consumers whose score ranged within a few points of your own.

Now that you understand the key factors that control your credit score. Know this also: the current status of your account is very crucial. Therefore, if you are falling behind with non-defaulted accounts (not exceeding four months past due), try contacting your creditor to see if you can restore those accounts and make them current again. However, if your accounts are already in collections or charged off, try to negotiate as your next course of action.

Remember not to worry about the "settled for less" warning that shows up on your credit report when your accounts are already past the due date, and your score already is affected. Know that you can always raise your score when you pay off all current creditors promptly and every negative account.

CHAPTER 3

Who Can See Your Credit File?

This Chapter Lectures About:

- Learn About the Permissible Purpose Protections
- Can Your Employer See Your Credit Reports?
- What's Needed In Order To See Your Reports?

One question that should always be in the back of your mind is: who is eligible to receive and review my credit report?

Often it feels like any and everybody can get access to your private financial information. Moreover, the mail that floods your inbox and mailbox is a result of some strangers accessing your credit report. These emails and letters include pre-approved offers for auto loans, mortgages and credit cards—all thanks to the prescreening services provided by the credit reporting agencies (CRAs) to these lenders and creditors.

Knowing this, it is time for you to know your rights about who and who should not be looking at your report.

Permissible Purpose

Surprisingly, just about anybody can receive your consumer credit file on the condition that their purpose for asking is validated by the Fair Credit Reporting Act (FCRA) statute's broad language. The usual suspects requesting for your credit report are current creditors, prospective creditors attempting to sell you more credit, current employers and future employers. Just about anybody covered under the "permissible purpose" can request to receive it.

Additionally, several reports have shown correlations between the credit report of a consumer and the risk that consumer can be to an insurance agency. Therefore, most insurance providers, especially automobile and homeowner insurers, have begun reviewing your report before any coverage can be issued. Thankfully, several state regulators have curtailed when and how an insurance agency can use your credit report against you. Be sure to get in touch with the insurance commissioner in your state if you felt there was an increase or denial of your insurance coverage was because of your credit report.

Below is a link of Section 604 of the FCRA which lawful defining purpose. It is worth a read to know who and who are eligible to get your personal information.

http://bit.ly/FCRALINK

Employers

It is common knowledge that it is illegal for employers to discriminate based on race, age or sex. However, you may not be hired if the employer does not find your credit report acceptable. So your bad credit is not protected by the law. That is why it is crucial to be forward-thinking whether you are currently an employee or aiming to work in specific industries, like securities and banking. Bad credit may also affect your occupation as an independent contractor or even your application for a professional license. So the state of your report can influence whether you can become a construction contractor, loan officer, insurance agent or attorney.

"How does credit history correlate with job performance?"

THE REASON IS SIMPLE: before a candidate can be considered for a role in a company, serious employer's nationwide use extensive evaluation processes. These processes include criminal background checks, reference verification and, of course, credit checks. Moreover, since corporate theft (bribery and embezzlement) has been around since the beginning of time, businesses will go through any legal length to shield themselves. So the law permits employers to use their judgment in determining the financial integrity and honesty of a candidate.

But before potential employers can perform a credit check on you as an applicant, they must first obtain your written authorization. While your standard credit file does not include your driving and criminal record, it is pertinent that you carefully read the authorization before signing. Such documents may as well cover access to receive copies of you credit records also.

Know that you have the right to deny the request of any person that wants to obtain your copies of your background checks, including your credit report. In reality, when you permit an employer to inquire about your report and it comes up negative, you may not be given the job. Since you cannot afford to lose a great job opportunity, your only way out of this situation is to allow the investigation into your credit; then you can try to explain your adverse credit information.

Note that allowing an inquiry into your credit score for employment does not in any way affect your reports. All you want is a job—not a credit extension.

Now you know that when applying for a job, you should read carefully any written permission that concerns obtaining your credit report before signing. Also, check if the document grants the employer permission to obtain your credit report at some point in the time in the future. While a good job is hard to pass up, be sure that you're okay with your employer continuously monitoring your financial and personal activities.

Illegal Requests for Your Credit Report

The FCRA's law on permissible purpose is extensive for anyone seeking to obtain your credit file. Nevertheless, there are certain instances where pulling your credit report by anyone is prohibited. Here are two instances:

1. Lawsuits

Let us say you are involved in a lawsuit; it is illegal for another party to request or use your credit file just because of that. Simply put: a terrible credit score cannot be used to prove to a jury or judge that you have fraudulent intentions or are desperate for cash; it cannot be used to prove why you are involved in the lawsuit in the first place. This applies both to the party being sued and the party suing.

2. Judgments

After losing a case, the winning party cannot use your credit report to prove that you are capable of paying or that you have assets that can be seized to pay up reparations the court awarded to the winner of the case. The lawful purpose does not cover anyone obtaining your report in an attempt to view your types of accounts, address and other personal information just because a reward on a judgment is to be collected.

TIP: To sue somebody for illegally obtaining a copy of your report, your action must be filed within a two-year statute of limitation. The only way to file a suit after two years is to prove to the court that you have the right to a more extended period because the employer (or person) that obtained your report willfully and materially distorted their intention for pulling the report. For instance, if an employer or person lies to you concerning the reason for pulling your report. Of course, you would need a competent attorney in a case like this.

CHAPTER 4

Getting a Free Copy of Your Credit Report

This Chapter Lectures About:

- Getting Free Credit Reports from AnnualCreditReport.com
- How To Obtain Your Annual Report
- Consumer Myths and Truths by the FTC

After you have learned who is and who is not eligible to access your credit report, now it is time to know how to obtain a copy of your report. Even if you do not have any pertinent need for your report right now, or if it has been a long time since you have viewed them, you still should pull your report now.

Please recall that credit reporting agencies (CRAs) are not obligated to notify you when unfavorable information is being reported about you. This should drive you to check out your report a month or two before making any major life changes, like applying for a new home mortgage or a new job. Also, before you tie the knot, make sure to review your report—this will be elaborated upon in Chapter 13.

Thankfully, as stated in Chapter 1, you are legally you eligible to a free copy of your credit files, according to the FACT Act, once a year from the main three (Equifax, Experian, and TransUnion) CRAs.

"So how do you pull these reports?" you ask. The answer is the officially sponsored website created by the Big Three CRAs in accordance to the FACT Act: AnnualCreditReport.com. Visiting this website is the fastest and most straightforward way to retrieve your credit report. While several web ads and infomercials may claim to provide free credit reporting to you, they would attempt to sell you other services or products if you go along on with them. Just go straight to the website—its interactive web pages are designed so that you can check each file from the three CRAs. Because the reports are not compiled, you will be requesting three different files from each bureau. Moreover, because these CRAs don't share information with one and other, carefully arrange all your three files in the right order. If you are married, be sure to get his or her reports, too. The sooner you begin, the better for you.

Since websites go through frequent updates, be sure to follow the instructions on the home page.

At the time of this publication, the first step at AnnualCreditReport.com is select a button that says "**Request your free credit reports**" or "**Request yours now**." Next, you are taken to a page where you have to 1) **Fill out a form**, the next page 2) **Pick the reports you want:** and 3) **Request and Review your reports online.**

In the "**Fill out a form**" section, you will need to provide your legal name, birthday, social security number (and verify it), and current U.S. Address. If you have lived in your current address for less than two years, you will be asked to fill in your previous address. In the "**Pick the reports you want**" section, you can separately select one of the CRAs (Equifax, Experian, or TransUnion). In the "**Request and Review your reports online**" section, before getting your credit reports, you will be asked more security questions that guarantee you are whom you say you are, ensuring nobody else can get your credit information. Be sure to print your credit reports so you can look at them later.

Remember, repeat these steps for each credit bureau.

Each CRA will request what level of credit report service you want. Be careful here if you don't wish to opt in for a one-a-month monitoring service—just select "**report only**."

You do not need to opt-in for a consumer comparative rating analysis or monthly monitoring services or even request your score. You will usually always have to spend a little cash on obtaining your credit scores. Just be careful when you are choosing a service on this website; you only have to pay for your score not the reports, so do not let these CRAs bamboozle you with some additional service or product you have to pay for.

Even though Congress made the accessibility of credit reports easy and free with the online platform, thousands of average consumers are still, in fact, spending dollars when they go online for their reports. While the copy of your report itself is free, CRAs have found ways to monetize the website by luring you to pay for some extra service or the other. Be careful when you request your report.

Get Your Annual Credit Report by Phone or Mail

Apart from a central website, the three CRAs also have a toll-free phone number and a mailing address where you can order your free reports without being solicited with other products and services. Unlike the online instant delivery method, the processing period and delivery time may take days. To order your report through your phone, call 1-877-322-8228. Then you will be prompted to follow the instructions of an automated menu to get your report delivered to you.

On your initial attempt to request for your credit report via mail, fill in the Annual Credit Report Request Form which can be found in the FTC Facts for Consumers brochure, then mail it to:

Annual Credit Report Request Service
P.O. Box 105281
Atlanta, GA 30348-5281

NOTE: According to FTC, it is not recommended for you to contact the three national CRAs separately. To get your report free of charge, your three options are to: visit AnnualCreditReport.com, call the toll-free line (1-877-322-8228), or via mail to the address above (Annual Credit Report Request Service).

TIP: Although you have obtained copies of your report within the last year, you are still eligible to get another free copy if a negative remark on your report impacted the result of an application. Instances like these may be denied credit, rental housing, insurance or employment. Also note that if you are presently unemployed and preparing to apply for a job within 60 days, or if you are a recipient of public assistance, or if you were defrauded, or if your creditor cut down your credit limit because of an issue occurring on one or more reports, you are also eligible to get another free copy.

TAKE NOTE: on your initial attempt to request for your credit report via using the Annual Credit Report service, there is the likelihood that one or more of the CRAs might not release your file. For instance, they may be claiming that you answered some of the personal security questions incorrectly online or, when it comes to a mailed request, that copy of your social security card was illegible. Therefore, to clear up the "errors," they will request for more items of identification, like your driver license or proof of current mailing address.

Sadly, in this case, this can become a problem. The issue is, any information you give the CRAs can be included on your credit file. However, the CRAs are not legally permitted to obtain your driving record, and no rule obliges them to include your driver license number on your credit file. So if you have to send you are a copy of your driver license, blur out some digits of your number. Your date of birth and address are enough proof to verification, as long as this information correlates with the existing information reported on your credit file.

If you do not want your phone number to be put on your report, never use your telephone bill as proof of your identity. However, if you want to safeguard yourself from credit fraud, like identity theft, providing your number in your credit file will allow lenders to contact you in case someone attempts to steal your identity. Remember, your phone number is just a minor precaution against identity theft and fraud—you still have to be more compact in protecting yourself.

For more on identity theft, see Chapter 15.

FTC Facts for Consumers Brochure

The Federal Trade Commission (FTC), the governing body of the Fair Credit Reporting Act and the Fair and Accurate Credit Transactions Act made a brochure (six pages) to assist consumers to know how to obtain their credit reports once in every 12 months for free. While most of the details have been covered in this guide, you may like to check it.

CHAPTER 5

Reading Your Credit Reports

This Chapter Lectures About:

- Keep Your Personal Information Personal
- Your Employment Information
- Credit Reports - They Are Keeping Score
- What You Should Know About Public Records
- Collection Account and How They Report
- All About Revolving Credit
- What is an Installment Loan
- How Mortgage Account Report
- Inquiries And Their Impact To Your Credit

Upon receiving the three credit reports and comparing them, you will see that they all have different layouts and formats. The reason is that the major three credit reporting agencies (CRAs)—

(TransUnion, Experian, and Equifax)—are independent of each other. As already stated, each organization is operating on its own. So whatever information received and maintained on you by them will differ. Even when all three CRAs get the same information from a creditor, they may update the data in time or manner that has variations. For instance, one glaring inconsistency is when different balances for the same account appear on all three credit reports.

As the years go by, there have been some meaningful improvements in the CRAs' formats. So the reports provided straight from all three CRAs presently are reasonably readable and understandable. However, it is the reports from third-party services (like the one received directly from a mortgage broker, car dealership or potential lender) that may particularly seem to bring some confusion. The reason is that they are purposely drawn up for the processing procedures of their application for quick lending decisions. Therefore, you have to remember that while your date may be formatted differently, the information is unchanged.

Your Personal Information

Consist of legal name, aliases (if any), date of birth, address history and social security number—will appear on all reports. Bear in mind that you have to check this information to fish out any inaccuracies, for this is the way credit files get indexed. A corrupted file (one with inaccurate or missing information) may bar the pulling of your file when needed, thus leading to your potential employer or creditor seeing "no record found." This is particularly serious if there is an inaccurate piece of information in your address, name or social security number. Reasonably, a majority of creditors will not waste time in checking your claim of having a verifiable credit file if they cannot find it on their first try.

Employment Information

There is a good reason why employment information is found on your credit files. The IRS does not report this information, Department of Labor or the Social Security Administration—your creditors report it. Although not every report contains your employer name, however, if you put your current employer's name when completing a credit application, there is a strong likelihood the creditor may report this to the CRAs. However, there is no need to bother yourself if your employment information does not appear on your credit reports. Besides, a majority of creditors consider this piece of information deficient and outdated. The fact is that creditors who make employment verification a requirement understand that they should directly reach out to your workplace instead of depending on what is or is not being reported in your credit file.

Scoring Your Credit Score

Your credit score—the renowned three digit number that signifies the chances of you falling behind on your payments come the next two years. To know if your credit is bad, average or high, you can order your score alongside reports. Moreover, upon reviewing your score, remember, do not cry or beat yourself up about whatever scores the CRAs come up with it. If your credit number is not as good as you want, thankfully, this guide will help you better it with just a little effort from your part.

Public Records

The information contained in this section of your report is obtained from the county, state and federal courts and includes bankruptcies, civil judgments, and tax liens. The format once again will vary, but the data typically includes a filing date, case number, case type, jurisdiction, balance, and other relevant details.

Collections

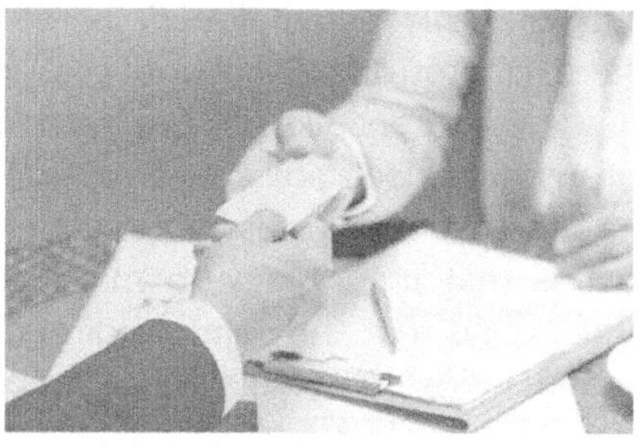

The "Collections" section of your report signifies to any accounts that have been assigned or sold to collection agencies because the original creditor was unable to collect the purportedly unpaid amount. However, some creditors have an internal collection department. Therefore, you may see the original creditor recorded in this section as well. Your account number, the current status of the account (showing if or not the debt remains unpaid, has been paid, or is being paid), an owed balance, and date of last activity (DLA) will be reported in this section.

Revolving Accounts

In this section, accounts listed as "tradelines" are primarily revolving. Just put: upon charging against the account, available credit decreases while the balance increase. Upon making a payment, the available credit then increases while the balance decreases. The revolving pattern will keep on repeating for the account's lifespan. A revolving account may be in the form of credit cards, gasoline cards, and department store cards: all these have the most significant effect on your credit score (we will talk more of this later).

It is quite simple to interpret this section of your credit report:

- Just start with the creditor's name.
- Reported or updated account.
- Date of the last activity.
- When the account was opened.
- How much credit was ever used.
- Projected monthly payment needed for account to remain current.
- Balance.
- Historical status (which shows how many recorded 30-, 60- and 90-day late payments).

Installment Accounts

Different from credit cards, the tradelines in this section are not revolving. A fixed loan amount is needed to open them, and a fixed payment is required every month until the balance gets to zero. After full payment, the account is then shut down and can never be reopened again. Installment accounts may come in the form of car loans, personal loans, and student loans.

Although these accounts are formatted the same way with revolving accounts, the primary distinction is that the payment made every month is set—not fluctuating like that of credit cards (where you are only obligated to pay your outstanding balance at the end of each statement period each month).

Mortgage Accounts

Here in this section, you can view every mortgage-secured accounts. Obligations included here are refinance and purchase mortgages, including home equity lines of credit and loans.

Inquiries

Whether a collection agency is pulling up your report to assess you or applying for credit, this inquiry will always be recorded and reported to other creditors for two years however, will only affect the score for one year. The inquiry then disappears from the record of that the two-year limit.

Wrapping up this chapter, you should now have rudimentary know-how of how to read every credit report section. While the data may be in varying formats and even labeled differently in all the three CRAs, keep in mind that the concept remains unchanged.

CHAPTER 6

Understanding the Credit Repairing Dispute Process

This Chapter Lectures About:

- ❖ Let See What Section FCRA 611 says
- ❖ If It's Inaccurate or Incomplete, You Must Delete
- ❖ FCRA Section 605 and Timeframes
- ❖ What's the Statue of Limitations for Outdated Info
- ❖ That's Not My Negative Information

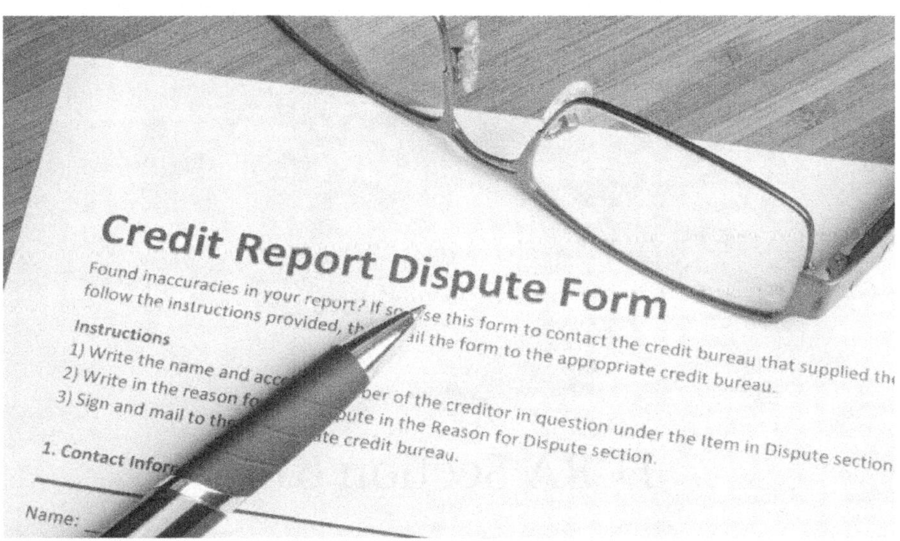

Now that you have learned the basics of your credit reports, you might have likely come across old, inaccurate or incomplete information on them. However, if these mistakes are negatively affecting your credit score, it is quite tricky urging with the notorious credit reporting agencies (CRAs) to find a quick and accurate fix for them. However, after the Fair Credit Reporting Act (FCRA) was enacted, consumers can do this with a little more ease. According to one of FCRA's provisions, you have the right to ask the CRA to correct any errors and by doing this, you initiate a "dispute."

Accordingly, the CRA is obliged to reach out to the original creditor and provide you with one of two solutions within 30 days. However, the CRA is not required by law to correct or change something in your file if the original creditor verifies the information on your file as correct. The CRA can make modifications to your report per your request (sending you a free updated copy) only when the original creditor agrees the information was incorrect or makes no attempt to provide an answer. The Two main FCRA sections (Section 611 and 605) govern the dispute process. The primary aim of this chapter is to explain these sections as well as how they cover your rights as a consumer. The next chapter ("Writing the Dispute Letter") will then show how to use the information received from this chapter.

FCRA Section 611

FCRA Section 611 explains the "Procedure in case of disputed accuracy," which states that "incomplete" or "inaccurate" information or information that "can no longer be verified" must either undergo modifications in accordance to the outcomes of the reinvestigation or must be "promptly" deleted from your credit report. Another provision of Section 611 states that "a reasonable amount of time" is given to the CRA to conclude your investigation. Additionally, according to the Federal Trade Commission and case law, that reasonable amount of time has been translated to 30 days for most cases.

NOTE: The word "reinvestigate" is used by the FCRA to define your first dispute process, like they had investigated something before then—when in fact there was no investigation from the start. The popular theory is that all three CRAs were aboard when the FCRA was drafted. Why not? Since the CRAs are big-time Washington lobbyist. So maybe they wanted to create the impression that any reported information on your credit file is investigated immediately from the very start. Now you know that it is not investigated or reviewed.

An excerpt of Section 611 is shown below. Although it is quite extensive, it is vital to this chapter because it outlines several of your rights. However, if you have the time to pour through, the key points of the excerpt follow the documents.

http://bit.ly/FCRALINK

Incomplete or Inaccurate Information

After reviewing your reports, there is a chance that you will come across several errors which will include inaccurate or incomplete information. However, do not worry, the process of repairing your credit requires patience and anyone promising you quick credit repair is only conning you out of your cash. All you have to do is to be smart and specific about it. Your goal is to correct or delete negative information from your report.

But, before beginning the dispute process, you must first identify the accounts or items that are possibly harming your score.

In the case of revolving accounts, if an account is still joined to the original creditor (not in collections somewhere or charged off), cautiously check out your payment history. Leave the account as it is if the balances are exact and the payments are on time.

Then, start searching for accounts that still are joined to their original creditors but with late payment reporting from some many years back. Identify these accounts—they could be 30-, 60-, or 90-days late or even more mainly only search accounts within the last two years. If you still have canceled stubs, checks or other receipts of payment, check to verify whether you have made those payments on time. In case you cannot find any old stubs, checks or statements, use your memory and try to remember—it is not against the law. Try to recollect as to whether you paid those accounts when they were due but the reports says that you were late. The credit report must say that you were "never late" if you were timely with payment on those accounts. Unlike accounts that read "deleted" or "removed," your credit score will be a whole a lot better if your account that is reported never past due..

The next step is to search for charged-off accounts or collection accounts. It is essential to know that it is impossible to make charged-off accounts or collection accounts current again. To improve your score in a situation like this, the best course of action is to delete these accounts like they were never even there. Try to sniff out any error in their reporting. According to the law, an inaccuracy can occur on any account provided that there is a mistake found in the listing; this mistake could range from an inaccurate listing of account ownership (like listing your account as the primary whereas you are only an authorized user) to the wrong account number. Bear in mind, that you have no legal obligation to help the CRAs change or amend a "typo". They have the legal obligation to report information about you accurately. Moreover, whatever you do, if reported charged-off accounts or collection accounts are not yours, always point it out the CRAs.

Ninety percent of the time, you will likely come across an error or two when going through your reports. Of course, you can correct any inaccuracy "promptly," within 30 days from when the consumer initiates the request, thanks to the FCRA.

You Must Dispute These Items If Inaccurate

When reviewing your reports, look out for the inaccuracies in the information below:

- Name misspellings
- Wrong date of birth
- Incorrect addresses
- Outdated information
- Incorrect account numbers
- Accounts that have been re-aged
- Incorrect balance
- Incorrect opening date
- Incorrect credit limit
- Credit card account not reporting credit limit
- Incorrect account type
- Charge off that has been sold or transferred has past due balance instead of zero balance
- Charge-off account showing currently past due
- Open charge-off accounts
- Accounts not included in bankruptcy
- Collection accounts with a credit limit
- Closed accounts reported as open
- You are reported as the owner of the account, when you are actually just an authorized user
- Accounts that are incorrectly reported as late or delinquent
- Incorrect date of last payment, date opened, or date of first delinquency
- Same debt listed more than once (possibly with different names)
- File merging or identity mix-up (your name may be similar or the same of someone else)
- Reinsertion of incorrect information after it was corrected
- Accounts that appear multiple times with different creditors listed (especially in the case of delinquent accounts or accounts in collections)
- Reinsertion of incorrect information after it was corrected
- Incorrect accounts resulting from identity theft

A comprehensive meaning of "inaccurate" is not provided by Section 611 of the FCRA. Sadly, if your dispute letter (discussed in the following chapter) says an account or item is "inaccurate," you would probably not get a useful reply from the CRA. What you need to do is to either point the error with a straightforward "does not belong to me" or deliver a comprehensive correction if the details would increase your score.

A short example: Look at the case of the account number of charged-off or collection item that is incomplete (missing a digit or two) or incorrect. If you write them a letter pointing out an account number error, the CRA will never modify past due payments nor erase the account. Instead, the CRA will probably correct the account number on your behalf, mainly when you have provided the accurate number. However, if that same account number is in no way similar to the account you have on record, your best move is to say that the account is not yours.

Keep in mind that an account can be tagged "inaccurate" for several reasons. Carefully search for errors in all nooks and crannies—from the title of your accounts to payment history to the balances to your dates.

FCRA Section 605

Section 605 of the FCRA, named "Requirements relating to information contained in consumer reports," states that out-of-date accounts and items must be deleted like they were never in existence. Luckily, the FCRA has a definite and legal time frame before an item can become obsolete. According to an FCRA provision, after seven years, negative information is not allowed to remain on your report. However, there some exemptions to this rule.

Exemptions to the FCRA Seven-Year Rule:

- Any credit inquiry has a lifespan of two years on your report.
- Bankruptcy dispositions can last up to a decade.
- Unpaid tax liens can remain on your report forever.

In the CRAs' contract with their source members, there is a specific disclaimer that warns their subscribers that they cannot and do not assure that the information found in any consumer file is accurate or complete. So should subscribers unsuspectingly depend on an inaccuracy in the files of consumers, the CRAs have freed themselves from paying hefty refunds. Just like a car salesperson offering you a car without assuring it will start.

To know precisely what your rights under the FCRA on the subject of outdated information, consider the four-page excerpt of Section 605 below.

http://bit.ly/FCRALINK

Obsolete Negative Information

As stated in Section 605 of the FCRA, adverse information cannot remain on your report after seven years. This information covers trade items like mortgages, installment loans or revolving accounts. Let us say you fell behind on your car loan some nine years ago and have not ever since been current, no evidence of lateness should be on your report—like it never existed. Now to repair your credit report, your next move is to search for obsolete adverse items.

However, because client subscribers pay their CRAs to report submitted information, they would prefer the information to remain indefinitely. Moreover, regarding your installments and revolving accounts, the law provides that negative information cannot be reported after seven years. As regards to a collection agency, your seven years start counting down when the collection agency accepts your account or after 180 days since you ceased paying to the original creditor. Concerning a charged-off debt, your countdown begins in the month the creditor reports the account as a profit and loss on an official record.

The problem here now is determining if these dates correspond to the ones on the record of your credit report. It is very likely that a collection agency may start worrying you several months before choosing to notify the CRAs.

However, even in today's automated climate, you would guess that the CRAs could precisely and effortlessly monitor obsolete information, thus updating all reports. In reality, that is never the case. Like the inaccurate information likely to pop up on your report, old items may continue to hang around for several years even after their expiration date. To delete stale information and uphold your rights, you have to keen on monitoring when the countdown starts Also referred to as "statute of limitations." The statute of limitations starts on the date of last activity (DLA) on your account.

The last time at which any financial activity is reported is called DLA. Let us say the DLA for a loan or credit card would be the date the account was closed or paid off. However, your payments history (over the past two to three years) affects your score—and you do not wish to delete good-standing accounts just for the reason that they have aged past seven years.

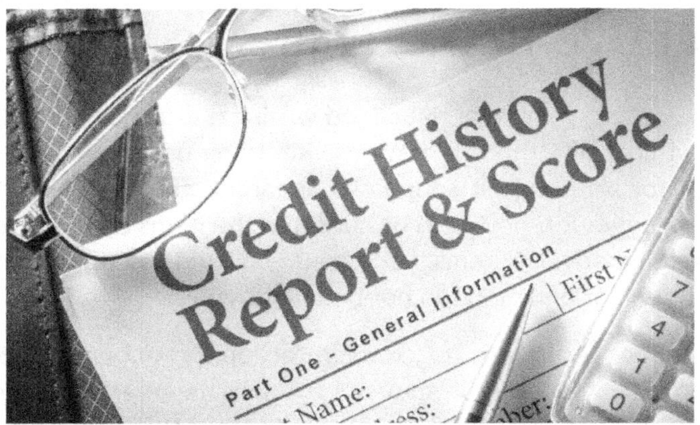

Outdated items you must dispute

Below is a list of obsolete items you may want to review:

- Charged-off accounts
- Place-for-collection accounts
- Bankruptcy
- Paid tax liens
- Paid judgments
- Paid child support reporting to be overdue

While these DLAs and time limits seem complicated, it is vital that you understand that old items are the fastest and easiest to get rid of from your credit report. The reason is that CRAs have the independent authority to delete items they consider stale too. Sometimes the CRA does not go through the trouble of sending the creditor a verification letter before it deletes a stale item. So if you know the DLA of your account has aged past several years—(even when your credit file is showing it as four years old), you are legally entitled to start a dispute and be optimistic that the CRA deletes it without sending a verification letter to the creditor.

You will not make headways sending a letter to the CRA arguing the date an active account was changed from default to charged-off, etc. Note that an account placed-in-collections or charged-off can never be converted back to current. The smart thing to do in this case to tell the CRA that the DLA of that account has aged past seven years. That is it—it is the job of the CRA to carry out the investigation.

Negative Items That Are Not Yours

Before exercising your legal rights and writing a dispute (as will be covered in the next chapter), there is another vital thing on your credit report you must look for. Although it sounds so apparent, the very first thing to do after receiving your report is to be sure that the items on it are yours. Apart from reviewing adverse items, you should be trying to figure out the items and accounts that belong or do not belong to you.

If you notice a pattern of foreign accounts or unrelated personal information (to you or your spouse or family member), you are probably viewing "foreign information" or "foreign accounts." This CRAs calls this occurrence "overlapping" or "merging." Simply put, the report on the credit file of another consumer has been mixed with yours. If you ever face this, it is necessary for you to find how to separate the correct information from your file. Get yourself out of the mix even if the other person's account is paid off or current. Even if the foreign account looks better than yours remove it. Holding on someone else's account is a problem because you could never judge their future payment history.

In a case like this, initiating a dispute for each account separately may lead to nothing. The smart thing to do is write the CRA, explaining the wrong merger of another person's credit history with your report. You may need to do a careful outline of the issue to the CRA. Alongside your dispute letter, for example, attach a printed copy of your credit report where you have circled or highlighted all the unrelated information.

The CRAs are not legally obligated to make use of "reasonable procedures" to guarantee the best level of information accuracy on your report. The truth of the matter is that as source creditors report your information to CRAs (whom then go on to process it), validating evidence is not required by the CRAs to verify the accuracy. Therefore, it is the job of CRAs to confirm the information and update it independently.

Tip: You can legally ask for the CRAs for an investigation if you want to verify something, or if you are unsure about the condition or existence of any item or account. Do not be held down: make the move and ask. In Chapter 7, you will see how you can exercise your rights (taught in this chapter) and write a dispute letter.

CHAPTER 7

Writing the Dispute Letter

This Chapter Lectures About:

- The CRAs And The Different Types of Verification Forms Used
- What You Need To Know About Manual Fill-In Forms
- Winning a Battle Or Winning A War - Picking Your Disputes
- Learning How To Prepare Your Dispute Letter
- Examples Of Various Disputing Methods
- The Best Way To Send Disputes
- How To Respond To a CRA Disputes Response

Removing adverse information from your credit report is the most vital step when trying to improve your score on a short-term basis. As stated in the previous chapters, credit reporting agencies (CRAs) are not obligated to give notification when adverse information is being reported about you. Upon receiving your information, the CRAs' only job under the law is to use their "reasonable procedures" to validate accuracy. However, there is no proper and detailed explanation of these procedures, like a list of what must be performed. Of course, if the CRAs were legally required to corroborate every piece of information they receive, they will burn out and shut down.

CRAs Verification Forms

The FCRA tries to balance the game for consumers with the dispute process. The dispute process gave the CRAs so much work, so they opted to restructure their dispute process—so they designed and provided a dispute form for consumers and separate verification forms for their source creditors.

Unsurprisingly, completing and returning verification forms are easier for creditors. Moreover, because the CRAs have 30 days to answer to your dispute, either to verify or correct an item, creditors are given a few weeks to return the CRAs the verification forms. However, bear something in mind: not every source creditor will turn around these forms within the allotted period—some will not even return it, at all. Just because of this, several disputes will bring about items being corrected or deleted.

Fill-In Dispute Forms

Below is an example of a multiple choice dispute options:

[ ] The account/item is not mine.

[ ] The account status is incorrect.
[ ] The account/item is too old to be included in my report.

When trying to initiate a dispute using the online platform, a pop-up may come to ask you if you want to dispute an item. Just select "yes" to continue. This is just a protection clause used by the CRAs to trick you into thinking that it is illegal to dispute an item the CRAs consider as valid or correct. Scale through their scare tactic and do not be intimidated. Just know that it is under the law for you to dispute any inaccurate information or item.

If you requested for your reports to be sent via email, among the documents will be a dispute form. The CRAs will advise to fill this already typed form only if there are any inaccuracies on your report. The funny thing is that these mailed dispute forms are simpler to complete because of two reasons:

1) Broadcasting their conformity to the legally required dispute process gives them more acclaim.
2) Supplying their forms is more convenient for them—because, with these simplified forms, their trained agents can swiftly read and convey the information on to their creditor verification forms.

If you have simple disputes (listed in a box or a line on the form), you can either use the online or mailed disputes forms. However, if your issues are complex or lengthy and cannot fit into the allotted space or there are not enough options on the document to address all your dispute issues, you may need to write the CRAs.

Concerning the mailed fill-in dispute forms, be cautious when filling them out as they may ask you to give out more personal information to the CRAs than you need to. The CRAs asking for more information does not mean you have to provide it. Just remember that if a fill-in dispute form does not adequately help your case, the best course of action is to write your letter.

Save Your Energy

Some inaccuracies on your report do not affect your rating. Common sense is needed when initiating a dispute—do not waste all your strength on the small or inconsequential things.

Let us say you want to remove a collection account from your file; don't bother with whether your report correctly shows your address as "Block #3" rather than "Unit 3." Alternatively, on the other hand, if your real name is Peter and what it reflects on your report is "Pete," or "Peterson—these harmless errors do not affect your score. Tackle the major issues first.

According to statistical data, apart from making use of a middle initial, consumers say they prefer using one form of their name for formal or essential documents, like credit applications. So nobody will ever know why the CRAs are still claiming to report received information when they keep messing up data.

There is a theory that those "harmless" parts of your report are not carefully monitored by CRA agents because they have lesser liability in cases of mistakes. So if you feel like ignoring something, do it. Moreover, if you eventually change your mind, you can always dispute it later.

Now place your attention on the critical personal information section. Keep all information accurate like your social security number (SSN) and date of birth (DOB). If you see "other" social security numbers linked with your identity, it may be for fraudulent uses. So you need to ask the CRAs to remove the wrong one.

If you need your report for insurance coverage, job or a loan, a wrong date of birth can become a big problem. Simply put, if your report says you are 20 years older or younger than you indeed are, there would be a delay in approval because more time would be needed for correct age verification. There have been times that a CRA wrongly reports that an applicant was dead even when he or she is alive and has current accounts. In cases like this, creditors suspect foul play and stop an application processing from investigating the matter.

How to write your Own Dispute Letter

After organizing all your items, you can write your letter, but make sure to put your disputes in one correspondence. It does not matter if you have a long list of disputes. You can arrange your disputes on multiple pages and in different ways.

For instance: in the left column, list all your accounts; in the right column, list the issues in a few words ("not my account," "always paid on time/never late," etc.). Alternatively, you explain your dispute first, then list the accounts associated with the issue. For example: "the following accounts do not belong to me..." Just keep it short and straightforward.

When disputing an item with the bureaus you want to be sure that you have a valid reason and are requesting the correct items to be investigated.

Making sure that you are air tight in your dispute reasoning is important. You will find that dispute reasons will add validity to your future disputes. If you choose to hire an attorney to pursue legal actions the letters submitted may be called to be used in court.

Do yourself a favor and make sure you are using real dispute instructions with real reasoning behind them. What is meant by this, is that you want to make sure that if you are disputing an account and you do not have solid proof that it is reporting inaccurately or in error then leave some room to be wrong. If you come out and say - THIS ACCOUNT ISN'T MINE, then you are lying and are committing fraud (don't do that).

Inaccuracies

Here is a quick guide to help you quickly identify inaccuracies on a credit report. When you review an account on a credit report check for these errors and if there is an error then a dispute is in needed. However, if there are no errors noted then an investigation is in order.

Name: The name of the creditor is reporting. Some collection agencies do not show names on credit monitoring reports. It's hard to verify an account with no name.

Account Number: Make sure there is an account number listed and that it is not all edited out. Some credit reports will transpose account numbers into short versions. If it has odd characters and letters it is possible that the account number is wrong.

Credit Limit: If the credit limit on a revolving account is not reporting, it can cause significant damage to the debt ratio and potentially lower their credit scores. This should be disputed if there is no credit limit.

High Credit: The high credit gives insight into the account and the maximum amount the consumer has borrowed on this account. If there is no High Credit reported it can cause issues with future financing and approvals. This should be disputed if there is no credit limit.

Date Opened: Is the Date Opened is not reporting or reporting inaccurately it can have an adverse effect on credit scores.

DLA (Date of Last Activity): The DLA shows the date the last payment was made. This is a very important date because it affects the statute of limitations on the account being reported. If there is no DLA there is no proof the account is reporting within the allotted timeframes of the FCRA.

Account Type: This one little area can have a big impact on a consumer's credit score. It is common to find collections reporting as Charge Off or Default.

Balance: If the balance is wrong it harms the debt ratio and may even show an account as being over the limit.

Terms or Payment: Inaccurate payment amounts can cause consumer difficulties with getting approved for financing. If the terms or payment are inaccurate it can often lead to inaccurate debt to income ratios used for qualifying for financing.

Payment History: Identify the late payments and determine with the consumer if you need to dispute any late payments. Pay close attention to the payment history on Charged Off accounts, once an account has been sitting for a while it can have missed dates or gaps reported.

Date Reported: This part of the account is VERY helpful when escalating the dispute process to the 2nd or 3rd Round. It is telling you if an account has been update after a dispute. You can use this to point out if the bureaus actually investigated an account.

SOL: The statute of limitations is not reported on most credit reports. This is the amount of time an account can report on a consumer's credit report. 7 years from the Date of Last Activity (NOT THE OPENED DATE) for collections and accounts. 10 years or more for Public Records.

If you not have a specific reason and you cannot identify an inaccuracy, here are our recommended starting instructions:

Collections: Unknown/Please validate | Unknown company/Please validate

Late Payments: {Date of Late} does not seem accurate, this needs to be verified or corrected to show paid as agreed never late.

Charge Off: I do not agree with the charge off status on this account, this need to be verified or deleted.

Bankruptcy: The date filed (discharged, dismissed...whatever you want here) does not seem correct. Please correct or remove this account.

Tax Liens: The balance reporting does not seem accurate. This needs to be verified or deleted completely.

Judgments: The balance reporting does not seem accurate. This needs to be verified or deleted completely.

Personal Data (Name, SSN, DOB, Address, Employer): This is not my (personal data and needs to be deleted from my report.

Inquiries: I do not recall giving my authorization for this credit pull, please remove this.

TIP: The smart thing is to put all your disputes in your first letter. However, if you missed something, you can deliver a second letter 30 days later. If the CRAs get more than one letter from you within a short duration of time before they can verify the first one, they can choose to postpone your first disputes. They will say that because you have added new information, you will have to postpone their investigation of the first disputes. All you need is 30 days of patience. By then, you should have received the initial corrected report.

Sending Your Dispute Letter

When correcting information on your credit report, make sure it reflects with all three CRAs. Even when one or two reports do not show an error appearing on the other, be on the safe side by telling all of them about the error. Do it because the error might be a recent one and has yet to spread to other reports.

Even if you have not received all three reports, send a dispute letter to all three CRAs. Know that you are a consumer, so an error on one report could mean the same error is on other reports. It is not crime disputing with all CRAs. Of course, if you can start the dispute process with one CRA, you will not have much trouble doing with the others. When a CRA cannot find an error, it will respond with a letter informing you about it.

Whether you are using the CRA dispute form or drafting your dispute letter, use only certified mail with return receipt requested. While a CRA hardly claims not to have received your letter, sending certified mail is still best for your correspondence, especially in cases of pressing legal disputes like identity theft.

Call the CRA to know whether your dispute was received. Note that when talking with CRA agents, be careful not to give them the information you do not want to be included on your report.

The following is a list of CRA customer service phone numbers:

- **Equifax:** (800) 685-1111
- **Experian: (888) 397-3742**
- **TransUnion:** (800) 916-8800

As soon as a CRA gets your dispute letter, it notifies you, then informs you later of the completion of the verification process. You may get a response much sooner than 30 days—it all depends on the number of accounts you are disputing and the speed of at which source creditors give back the verification forms. Still, give it up to 40 days. If you do not get anything after 40 days, know that your dispute was not recognized, so send another one.

What's is found in a CRA's Response to a Dispute

After receiving your corrected reports, carefully read through them. The first or second page should include a paragraph stating the information reinvestigated upon your request, next is a list of affected accounts and the results of the reinvestigation. Here you will see one or more of the three possible outcomes regarding the dispute process:

1. **Deleted:** Deleted accounts—like they never existed.
2. **Verified—No Change: No changes were made. The accounts will continue to report an information**
3. **Update: This could mean one of three things:**
   I. Deleted late or past due indications.
   II. After the review of the account by the source creditor, a small adjustment was made, and it does not affect your report.
   III. Along with the forms, the source creditor returns an updated submission on your file (a requirement after every few months) to update your account. In this case, do not be fooled by the "update" notification, and make sure the first issue has been addressed. If not, send a follow-up letter.

CHAPTER 8

When the First Dispute Letter Fails

This Chapter Lectures About:

- How To Counter Punch With Your Second Dispute Letter
- The Facts Behind A 100-Word Consumer Statement
- Knowing When To Contact A Credit Professional
- The True Facts When It Comes To Suing The Credit Bureaus

ROUND 1

Bureau Dispute: Dispute Inaccuracies & Validity

ROUND 2

Bureau Dispute: Request documentation and investigate for inaccuracies and validity Creditor Direct Dispute: Ask for proof with verification and validations

ROUND 3

Bureau Dispute: Submit responses from the creditors

1) Bureaus didn't send proof, creditor didn't send proof: Ask for the Removal
2) Bureaus didn't send proof, creditor did send proof: Review proof for errors
3) Creditor didn't send proof: Ask for the removal or deletion
4) Creditor did send proof: Review proof for errors

After sending a dispute letter highlighting the issues on your credit report, you should likely get a corrected report after a month or so. However, one or two CRA may claim your disputes was accurately verified, hence no change to that adverse information.

Your next plan is to send another dispute letter.

Sending a Second Dispute Letter

Do not be let down by uncorrected reports. This time, write them again, sending a copy to the CRA's attorney.

If you cannot get the name of a CRA's attorney, send your letter to its legal department. While you might direct your letter to a real lawyer, it is actually the CRA's legal assistants that will read them. Your query should include to ask why they updated or removed some erroneous items or accounts and left others untouched. Include the remaining erroneous items in a list. You may just get a letter back from a CRA agent in the legal department—the letter will not come from the CRA's attorney.

In your second letter, you can legally demand that the CRA's legal department send more information concerning your disputes. These include:

I. A copy of the completed verification form used
II. The contact information (name, title and phone number) for the creditor's agent who completed the verification form.
III. A copy of the documents showing evidence of the debt

TIP: Do not stop pushing. Do not think you are "bothering" the CRAs with a second letter. The problem is that consumers fear retaliation in the form of the CRAs reinstating previously corrected information because a consumer kept "bothering" them. Do not give up!

Most times, a second, well-written letter will bring a more positive outcome. However if the CRAs do not delete or correct information upon your continuous requests, they may attempt to use your second letter as a "consumer statement." This means that they will put an entry beside the disputed item, like: "Account information disputed by the consumer (Meets requirements of the Fair Credit Reporting Act)." Do not let this notation appease you—it does not affect your credit score.

Sadly, by the third dispute letter the CRAs will probably try to reply with a firmer letter stating that your matter is no longer up for reinvestigation—plus saying it is legally "frivolous" and "irrelevant" and time-wasting. Your next move, in this case, is to take your matter to the Federal Trade Commission. The FTC's intervention may come after several months. Alternatively, hire a lawyer.

Tip: If you cannot afford a lawyer, call the Federal Trade Commission toll-free: 1-877-FTC-HELP (1-877-382-4357). Visit their website at www.ftc.gov or mail a letter to Federal Trade Commission 600 Pennsylvania Avenue, N.W. Washington, D.C. 20580.

100-Word Consumer Statement

When a continuous dispute does not work out in your favor, you are legally allowed—under the provision is found in Section 611 of the Fair Credit Reporting Act (FCRA)—to add a 100-word "consumer statement' on your report, serving as an explanation of your side of the story.

In truth, this statement does not affect your credit score. Still, the CRAs encourage many consumers to add it after failed attempts to resolve disputes. The statement is an "appeasing" technique and it may be useless because:

I. A personally submitted statement has no effect on your credit score or your creditworthiness.
II. There is less likelihood of a creditor reading it.
III. The smart thing is to explain in person to a potential employer or creditor the errors on your credit report with facts that back up your claims.

You have the right to a consumer statement. If you choose to write one, make it concise and straight to the point. Avoid stupid excuses or long stories; these may affect your credibility. While you can legally write "I do not owe this debt" as a statement, improve your legitimacy by using it in moderation and not with all your accounts. The best thing to do it explain why the negative information on your report was not your fault and not within your control.

Don't Explain All Negative Information In Your Statement

I. Medical bills that are showing as collection accounts because insurance has not covered them yet.
II. A bankruptcy that was dismissed, but your debts were not discharged.
III. Severe account changes due to divorce, major medical issues, death or identity theft.

TIP: It is good to always include a medical debt in your statement. Sometimes, medically insured procedures or visits remain uncovered due to one error or another. Hence, delayed medical payments. Moreover, even while you are still a patient at the hospital, your overdue bills can be sent to collection agencies in this case. Thankfully, once the insurance company pays the bill, the collector is legally required to delete the account from your report.

Talk to a Professional If Necessary

You must know your legal rights regarding your credit report. If trying your best does not work out, seek the assistance of a credit expert, an attorney, tax professional or accountant. Recently, many scammers came up with so-called do-it-yourself tricks to repair your credit for a small fee. The smartest thing to do educate is to yourself or seek a certified credit professional. If you are getting nowhere with your disputes and know that you are in the right, consider filing a lawsuit. Find an experienced attorney lawyer in the area of consumer rights and debtor/credit issues.

There are two types of consumer rights attorneys: litigators and non-litigators. A litigator is a lawyer with years of experience in the courtroom. A non-litigator (aka transactional attorney) has little experience in the courtroom and prefers settling out of court. Either type of attorney can begin to write letters on your behalf. Moreover, if after, you do not get any good news, take the CRA to court. Here, you have to be sure of the reputation, experience, and credentials of your lawyer.

Before Hiring a Lawyer

I. Notice how the office is ran? Is the staff professional, organized, helpful and friendly?

II. During the first consultation, ask the lawyers questions and see if he or she provides logical and realistic answers. Note that lawsuits come with advantages and disadvantages. If you lose a case, you may be charged to compensate the other party for their effort in defending the case.

III. Carefully read through the lawyer's retainer agreement. Bring it home and read through it thoroughly. If a lawyer does not give you a copy to read through ahead of time, it is best to find another lawyer.

Facts About Suing a Credit Reporting Agency

It is not unusual for CRAs to receive lawsuits from consumers and federal authorities for violations of the FCRA. As a consumer, to win a suit against a CRA, you have to prove that:

I. The CRA was asked repeatedly to correct inaccurate information;
II. The CRA was knowing negligent or noncompliant or negligent;
III. Damages were suffered due to the inactions and actions of the CRA (e.g., loss of favorable interest rate, wages, time, money); and
IV. The suit was filed within two years of the violation.

If you win the case, the FCRA states that CRA may automatically pay you up to a $1,000 in damages. Other real damages may be awarded, such as the payment of attorney's fee, court costs, and lost wages. It is a rarity and hard to prove, but there have been cases of payment due to willful infliction of emotional distress. In the case of intentional misconduct, a judge or jury can impose more damages of large sums as a punishment to CRA for bad conduct. This is also a rarity and should not be depended upon.

Sadly, lawsuits can drag on for months and even years. However, if you have a good lawyer, he or she will keep on writing letters on your behalf to potential employers, lenders and existing creditors as damage control.

CHAPTER 9

Dealing with Collection Agencies

This Chapter Lectures About:

- The Mechanics Of How Collection Agencies Work
- The Fair Debt And Collections Practices - Act And Who It Governs
- How Validation Of Debt Letters Works
- The Key Components To Include In Your Validation Letter
- Tips To Make A Collection Agency To Stop Calling You
- Stopping Collections Agencies From Calling Your Employer
- How To Win When Settling A With A Collection Agency

To discourage unfair debt collection practice, Congress enacts laws called the Fair Debt Collection Practices Act (FDCPA). This law applies to collection agencies, not to lenders or creditors.

Collection agencies have earned a bad reputation over the years. So you must learn to protect yourself from the harassment of collection agencies and the damages they can cause to your credit reports.

How a Collection Agency Works

Traditionally, creditors hire collection agencies to be the bad guy when payments have defaulted. To collect overdue payments from customers, original creditors make use of their internal collection department for a few months. Since chasing bad debt is costly and may affect the creditor's reputation, creditors hire a third party to do their dirty work, especially when the consumer seems like a hard nut to crack.

By working directly with the original creditors, collection agencies earn a cut of the payment or buy the debt at a good discount and keep the extra money obtained. Until you pay, collection agencies cannot make money, so they keep harassing you. Thanks to the Internet, you are very easy to find. Whether through your neighbors, friends, relatives or employer, they will find you and try to force you into paying them through intimidation or embarrassment.

The Fair Debt Collection Practices Act (FDCPA)

Because of the abusive ways of collection agencies up until 1977, Congress set the Fair Debt Collection Practices Act (FDCPA). In this Act, you have the right to fair treatment by a debt collector. Certain activities and methods of debt collection are firmly banned.

http://bit.ly/FDCPALINK

Validation of the Alleged Debt

Apart from their use of unfair methods of chasing debts, collectors are known for trying to collect more than they are permitted to. They even go after the wrong consumers, most times because they buy collection accounts with inaccurate records. According to the FDCPA, you have the right to verify any alleged debt for accuracy.

To validate an item or account on your credit report, the CRA has to contact and get information from the original creditor whose response determines the accuracy of that item or account. So, when dealing with a collection agency, you have the right as a consumer to initiate the validation process.

After getting the initial letter called a Dunning letter from an collection agency, you have within 30 days to write a letter to the agency. The collector will then reply with a letter stating that the debt is your responsibility and that it is entitled to collect the money either as the new owner of the account or on behalf of the creditor. Note that the collector has to stop all collection activity until it can show you this evidence. Inability to show the slightest evidence, the creditor must stop all collection activity and delete the collection account from your credit report.

If a lawyer or law firm calls or mails you in an attempt to collect debt, there are two likely possible situations are playing: Either the lawyer is playing the role of a collection agency, or he or she is hired to sue you if you do not pay promptly. According to the FDCPA, until a lawyer hired by a collection agency and/or creditor files a lawsuit against you, he or she is legally seen as a "collector" and must follow the same guidelines of a collection agency.

An Excerpt from the FDCPA Regarding Validation of Debts

FDCPA Section 809. Validation of debts [15 USC 1692g] (b) If the consumer notifies the debt collector in writing within the thirty-day period described in subsection (a) that the debt, or any portion thereof, is disputed, or that the consumer requests the name and address of the original creditor, the debt collector shall cease collection of the debt, or any disputed portion thereof, until the debt collector obtains verification of the debt or any copy of a judgment, or the name and address of the original creditor, and a copy of such verification or judgment, or name and address of the original creditor, is mailed to the consumer by the debt collector.

Under the FDCPA, know that you are being violated if the collection company tries to chase unverified debts or has not removed them from your credit report. In this case, you will be awarded a statutory sum of $ 1,000.

Even when you are not facing any harassment from a collection agency, you still need an FDCPA verification to truly know if you have collection accounts on your credit reports. Collection accounts, particularly old ones, have little to no effect on your credit score when compared to an original creditor in charged-off or default status. Therefore, removing newer collection accounts can significantly increase your points.

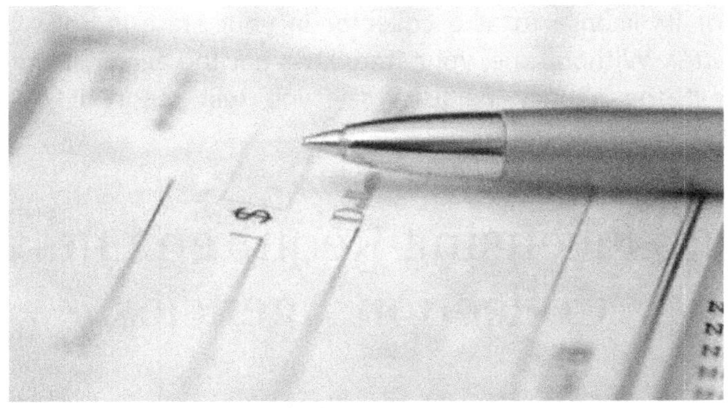

Writing a Verification Request Letter

To stop the harassment of a collection agency as well remove a collection account from your credit report, you need to write a letter asking for debt validation.

According to the Federal Trade Commission, a simple breakdown of an account (like a printed document or information on a letterhead) is not enough to validate a debt. You have to show to the collector that you require more evidence to prove the debt is accurate and legitimate—not just by word of mouth. So in your letter, you must request the following information:

I. **A document that proves the entitlement of the agency to the debt collection:** This is an assignment agreement or buy/sell contract between the collection agency and the original creditor—or between the latest collection agency and the previous one.

II. **Origination documents:** Original documents that show your signature on the agreement for services, loan application or credit card. A copy of your contract with the original creditor to prove whether the account could be initially assigned or transferred under the law to a collection agency or another creditor.

III. **Usage history:** You have the right to view a statement that breaks down your medical bill or payment history or credit card.

Do not forget to request a copy of the state and local licenses of the agency that grants its authority to act as a collector in your state. Often, an agency that is attempting to collect from you is from another state. Dig deep and find where that agency is from. If it is not from your state, add a request for its license to as a collector in your state in your verification request letter. Without one, your state laws bar the agency from collection activities. If the agency persists, say you will report it to the state authorities.

State Licensing Requirements for Collection Agencies

Alabama	License Required
Alaska	License and Bond Required
Arizona	License and Bond Required
Arkansas	License and Bond Required
California	No License Required
Colorado	License and Bond Required
Connecticut	License and Bond Required
Delaware	License Required
District of Columbia	No License Required
Florida	License Required
Georgia	No License Required (Only a Bond Is Required)
Hawaii	License and Bond Required
Idaho	License and Bond Required
Illinois	License and Bond Required
Indiana	License and Bond Required
Iowa	License Required in Certain Instances
Kansas	No License Required (Certificate of Authority Required in Some Instances)
Kentucky	No License Required If Collection Agency Is Paid By Creditor, Not Debtor
Louisiana	No License Required

Maine	License and Bond Required
Maryland	License and Bond Required
Massachusetts	License and Bond Required
Michigan	License and Bond Required
Minnesota	License and Bond Required
Mississippi	No License Required (Certificate of Authority Required in Some Instances)
Missouri	No License Required (Certificate of Authority Required in Some Instances)
Montana	No License Required (Certificate of Authority Required in Some Instances)
Nebraska	License and Bond Required
Nevada	License and Bond Required
New Hampshire	No License Required (Certificate of Authority Required in Some Instances)
New Jersey	No License Required (Only a Bond Is Required)
New Mexico	License and Bond Required
New York	License and Bond Required Only in the City of Buffalo
North Carolina	License and Bond Required
North Dakota	License and Bond Required
Ohio	No License Required (Certificate of Authority Required in Some Instances)
Oklahoma	No License Required
Oregon	License and Bond Required (Out of State Agencies May Be Exempt)
Pennsylvania	No License Required (Certificate of Authority Required in Some Instances)
Rhode Island	No License Required (Certificate of Authority Required in Some Instances)
South Carolina	No License Required (Certificate of

	Authority Required in Some Instances)
South Dakota	No License Required (Certificate of Authority Required in Some Instances)
Tennessee	License and Bond Required
Texas	No License Required (Only a Bond Is Required)
Utah	No License Required (Only a Bond Is Required)
Vermont	No License Required
Virginia	No License Required (Certificate of Authority Required in Some Instances)
Washington	License and Bond Required
West Virginia	License and Bond Required
Wisconsin	License and Bond Required
Wyoming	License and Bond Required

If a collection agency does not have your current address, do not give it to it. When requesting a debt verification, ask them to send the documents via your previous address (where it would be forwarded to you), a post office box number or a fax number. If it is a nearby agency, go and pick it up in person—if you are not worried that you would give out unnecessary information or become agitated.

Under the law, without adequate debt verification, an agency cannot:

I. Collect the debt (and sue you)
II. Contact you about the debt
III. Report the debt to the CRAs

Because a collection agency has only 30 days to respond to your verification request, send one copy of your letter via a mailing method that requires a signature upon receipt. After 30 days if the debt collector does not respond, quickly write back again. Now your second letter must make it clear to the collector that it has not provided you with the legally required documents, which is violating the FDCPA [explicitly, section 809(b)]. Demand that the agency stops all collection activities and deletes the collection account from all three CRAs—as it had never existed.

No matter the outcome of a verification process, or even if you did not request for verification, you could legally demand that the collector stops calling you. Under Section 805(c) of the FDCPA, you can ask the collection agency to cease all contact with you—both calls and letters.

Under the law, after receiving your letter, the agency can still send you one letter—a letter that agrees to cease collection activity, or telling you of its plans to sue you or repossess property used in securing the debt.

Prevent Them from Contacting Your Employer

Under a provision in the FDCPA, Section 805(a)(3), you can stop a collection agency from calling your employer when you make it clear that the employer prohibits such calls. You do not even have to write a letter to the collection agency to abide by this law, but for the case of documented proof, please do.

Settling with a Collection Agency

Even after stopping a collection agency from harassing you, your verified debt will remain on your report. To remove adverse accounts from your credit file, you have to negotiate settlements with the collection agency. In fact, the older the account, the higher the likelihood of the collector settling for less than the original amount of the debt. You can settle with a creditor-hired lawyer as well, but you will likely pay higher if the creditor has already won the lawsuit.

Either by writing or calling to the agency, you can make a settlement. Begin with a reasonable offer. An excellent place to begin is 20-30 percent of the total amount owed. It is a bad idea to ask for the creditor's initial offer—you would be working against yourself. Write a letter to the agency stating you will pay a settlement amount in return for the delinquency deleted or the collection account deleted from your report.

Because collection representatives earn their pay on commission, they will try to get as much as they can from you. They might say they will willingly update your report and clear it when you pay in full. Counter by saying that this it is not okay—that no matter how much settlement you choose to pay, you want the account gone.

Their first response is probably no; they might even claim that deleting real debts is illegal. Know that this is not right. They are only following their internal policy. No law stops them from removing an account from your file. Try to find a supervisor and negotiate directly with him or her to delete the account, and have them write it in a letter as well.

You can even tell them to ask the original creditor to delete the default indication or charge off from your report, too. They will claim that they are powerless to do that. Tell them that they must have some pull with the creditor since they got the account directly from the creditor.

In reality, it takes time for account representatives to start the account removal process, so they might not assure you a positive outcome. If so, ask to speak to a supervisor. If the supervisor does not yield, start your own dispute through the CRAs, then ask the supervisor whether he or she will at least be willing to ignore the verification forms arriving in a few weeks. This method, if the collection agency agrees, will span up to 45 days.

TIP: If the collection agency does not remove an account after you have paid in full. Dispute it with the CRAs—the agency will probably ignore the verification letter from the CRA in case of a paid-off account, hence clearing your debt.

It is true that it is never easy negotiating with a collection agency. Here are some few hints to get you through:

Contact the agency around month ending

After the agency has had your account for more than two or three months, wait just a few days before the end of the month before negotiating with it. Because during this time, the agency is trying to meet its commission quota and will take what it gets. Guarantee them an overnight check will be sent on a specific date, like on the 30th or 31st.

Offer one large lump sum

If you can pay the agency one large lump sum upfront, they will be more willing to remove the account from your file.

Make up one good story

No matter your initial offer, make it clear it is your best offer. For example: because you wish to spend your tax refund wisely, you lost your job, you have got a major surgery that will leave you bedridden for several weeks, etc.

Submit your offer in writing

Collection agencies secretly understand your demands and will never verbally negotiate those terms over the phone. However, a precise offer put in writing can make a difference. You can either fax them the offer or mail it to them.

Rather than writing your letter, request an already drafted one from the collector. They do this all time so it should not be a problem. Just careful go through the letter and make sure you are okay with the information and terms, from amounts to dates. If you do not like something, confidently make it clear and ask them for a re-write of the letter. Note that collector agencies are only desperate for cash and do not care about your report.

After sending your payment, contact the collector agency after a week to see if things are in order. First, to be sure that your payment was received and accurately credited to the account. Second, you must demand a "Release Letter." The agency might come up with a 30-day excuse but keep demanding for it once a while until you get it. This letter must state the date it was paid in full and that you have no additional obligations to the account. Make sure you protect this letter—it will come in handy in years to come.

Caution: No matter your settlement plans with the agency, always pay with certified funds or money order—not a credit card payment or personal check. If they can get your credit card number or check account over the phone, they can easily deduct future payments automatically! If an agency says, it will sue you if you do not quickly provide your payments over the phone, know that it is a trick. They can always wait for your overnight payments!

CHAPTER 10

Dealing with Secured Accounts That You Can't Afford

This Chapter Lectures About:

- How To Handle Vehicle Repossessions
- The Foreclosure Process and Procedures
- Students Defaults And Who You Should Contact
- Tax Liens and How They Could Be A Big Mess

Being an American, you are entitled to the American Dream: home, car, formal education and tax refunds. Sadly, you may lose all these if you do not live by the rules.

Repossession

Your vehicle or boat can be repossessed (taken away) if you are late on payments for it. After missing a payment, the lender sends you notification of the amount past due and accrued fees and interests. Sadly, you cannot ignore auto lenders because they can quickly take your ride.

YOUR OPTION IS TO EITHER:

1. Call your lender

Your lender may take partial payments for a time frame, or it might even run a program where you can transfer one or two month's payments to the end of the loan. Be sure to call them and confirm.

2. Consider voluntary repossession

After being notified of a past-due payment and you know you are unable to pay up, try voluntary repossession. To avoid sudden embarrassment or losing the personal belongings in your vehicle, call the creditor and tell them when and where the vehicle and keys will be available.

Unfortunately, voluntary repossession will reflect on your credit report and may still have financial obligations to the lender. The amount is known after your vehicle is publicly auctioned. Of course, you have to right to bid for your vehicle, but you still have to pay in cash—quite not realistic when you do not have the money, to begin with.

When it comes to vehicles on auction, the eventual buyer gets a good deal, and the creditor may not get back the full outstanding amount, which has also accrued more fees like auction expenses, storage, towing and interest. The difference between the sale price and currently owed debt is called "deficiency balance." (In case of a vehicle lease, deficiency balance can also be owed). Your lender might notify you of this outstanding amount and more probably send a collection agency after you.

If you think you can pay up days before your vehicle is repossessed, most lenders have an internal policy that can be of assistance. They might give you a pass on a two month's payment and then extend the loan payment by two more months—say you have a 30-month loan and two deferred payments, the lenders may extend the loan to 32 months. Call them and see if they can agree to your request. If so, they will draft a new contract or loan coupon book and mail it to you. They will likely consider this arrangement when you make clear of your financial issues before your delinquency is too far gone.

Keep in mind that this a secured debt. If your delinquency extends over 60 days, your vehicle will be repossessed.

Repossession equates secured debt. Creditors have the legal right of personal property confiscation as collateral for any debt.

When your vehicle has been repossessed, it is time to give your credit report a thorough review. Check the balance on it. There is a strong likelihood that the balance on your credit report does not equate to the amount the collection agency wants to get from you—as a result of alleged costs subtracted and added to the loan. It variation can come in very massive amounts.

In case of any inaccuracy, do not be afraid to dispute that item through the CRAs directly. When to is comes to any collection issue, if the creditor (as a current issue) does not have an account anymore, the likelihood of finding the needed documents for debt verification reduces as times go by.

Foreclosure

Foreclosure can happen weeks just after missing a mortgage payment. Do not waste time! If you are late on mortgage payments, start reviewing your finances.

In real life, most homeowners tackle the smaller bills before the larger one. In paying at least some bills, they enjoy the ease and sense of accomplishment. However, you have to set your priorities straight: would you rather lose your home or your cell phone? Just second to food to eat and healthcare, your mortgage should be a big priority.

Sadly, unless you can persuade the mortgage lender to draft a new contractual arrangement, it is useless to think of making a partial payment. Because even when your mortgage is $1 short, the lender can legally default the loan, drawing your closer to foreclosure.

Depending on your state, there is a variation in the process of foreclosure. However, most steps are simple. When a payment is missed, the lender reminds you of it and the amount you owe. If you cannot pay within a few more months (or make your account current), you will be notified that your account is scheduled for the foreclosure process.

Now, the lender will probably reject payments in the form of personal checks. Sending certified funds is the only sure way of "curing" the default and reinstating the loan. When unable to meet this obligation, the lender files a document with the court and applies for an order to auction your home.

Caution: If your home is covered by a deed of trust, in contrast with a mortgage, foreclosure can be much faster, depending on the state. With a deed of trust, the lender does not need the court to take back your home.

When the foreclosure process begins, a notice of sale is usually published in the local newspaper. However, before your house is sold, you still have the opportunity to persuade the lender to reinstate your loan. It is not easy, but it is possible!

Now the lender starts to "accelerate" your loan. Here you have to pay up the entire mortgage balance very quickly within the next couple of days!

To escape this issue, you can consider selling your home quickly by advertising the home for sale, showing it potential buyers, accepting an offer and finalizing the sale (at a "closing") all before your house is auctioned off.

Student Loans

Student loans will always come back to bite back in the years to come. After many decades after leaving school, many people are still paying students loans. Loans they thought would be cleared off by their future jobs.

First, when dealing with student loans, know what type of student loan it is. Some loans are financed directly by the schools (especially specialty or technical). This debt can be treated as a personal loan or revolving debt—they can be negotiated or even included in bankruptcy; these loans do not concern us much. The federal government probably insures privately sponsored student loans from big banks. As government lends, of course, it will also collect.

Federal student loan programs are quite lenient with borrowers. Always contact them when you fall behind in your payments. No matter old your loan is, you can enjoy benefits like deferment, forbearance or reduced payment arrangement. Just make it clear to them that you are having a hard time paying up, and they will provide you with less stringent options. Your loans can even be changed from collection to current status. Never ignore your student loan lenders or collectors for long. Doing so will only encourage drastic actions against you.

In the case of a defaulted student loan, it may remain with loan department for several months, or get passed to a collection agency or a litigation attorney—depending on the amount you owe and your efforts to contact the original lender or succeeding collector.

Note that the IRS can come in at any time. Because the IRS is a powerful federal body, it can hold on to your entitled tax returns until your debt—including penalties, fees, and additional interest—is paid in full. If you know that the IRS is keeping your tax refunds, ask your employer to increase your number of exemptions. He or she will give you a W-4 Form to fill. Consult your tax advisor or accountant to help you calculate the exemptions needed to increase your tax returns and pay off your debt.

In case of a deferred student loan, know how it is showing on your credit file. In case of any inaccuracy (showing deferment or forbearance status instead), write a dispute letter to the CRAs. A simple letter like this will do:

"My student loan account number *** is not in default—it is in a deferment status. Please correct this indication and mail me a copy of my updated credit report within 30 days... Thank you."

For further assistance, contact the Federal Student Aid Information Center at (800) 433-3243.

Tax Liens

Until your taxes are in a delinquent status and/or a lien has been filed against you, your taxes will not appear on your credit report. Whether personal or business, you risk the wrath of the IRS when you are late on your federal taxes. Learn to put the IRS first when it comes to your debt.

Even after paying your owed tax obligation, it can legally stay on your report for seven more years. For outstanding tax liens, they can stay in your report forever. Sadly, when you are behind on your taxes, the IRS can target other areas of your life—they can file a lien against your property and if necessary levy it.

A lien is a security for an outstanding tax, whereas a levy is an action of seizing property to fully or partially satisfy such lien. If you find an IRS lien on your report, a lien has been placed on one of your properties—probably your home. So when you sell that house, your debt needs to be paid up or paid with the sales proceeds.

You cannot even get a home equity loan or refinance to pay the IRS. After paying your current mortgage, the IRS is next in line to be paid. In some rare cases, to get paid, the IRS can strong-arm you to put your house on sale.

Your social security benefits, retirement accounts, proceeds from lawsuits, inheritance, money owed to you by others, vehicles, real estate, the monetary value of life insurance, income and bank account—all these can be touched by the IRS. When business taxes are owed, the all-powerful IRS can seize your business assets and business bank accounts. Because it is not bound by state laws, you cannot hide from the IRS. However, like with other creditors, you can plan and pay your taxes in installments. Note that small payments may only confuse both parties. Never sign anything the IRS agents tell you to. Before you do anything, get IRS-published rule called "Taxpayer Bill of Rights." If you know, you cannot practically pay off the IRS, quickly invest in an accountant or lawyer.

To formally submit a settlement offer to the IRS, an Offer in Compromise (OIC) is required. Because your financial life is wholly assessed, the OIC is a serious process. Of course, you would need an experienced lawyer or accountant if you chose to initiate this process.

CHAPTER 11

Bankruptcy: Why and Why Not to File

This Chapter Lectures About:

- ❖ What Is A Bankruptcy?
- ❖ Learning About The Different Bankruptcy Chapters
- ❖ When To Seek Help From A Bankruptcy Attorney
- ❖ The Damage A Bankruptcy Does To Credit Scores

You need a bankruptcy lawyer when you are being sued and your assets are being seized or your wages are being garnished. If you cannot file for bankruptcy, your lawyer can provide you with other options. Thanks to a change of laws and attitude, bankruptcy is nothing to be ashamed of.

Types of bankruptcy: Chapters 7, 11 and 13

United States Constitution (specifically Article 1, Section 8) places bankruptcies under federal jurisdiction with cases being filed in the United States Bankruptcy Court. However, each state has its law on which assets can be forfeited).

Under the Federal Bankruptcy Code, we have six types of bankruptcy (named as numbered chapters). However, three of the most popular ones will be explained here.

CHAPTER 7

A Chapter 7 bankruptcy is called "liquidation," and it can apply to businesses or individuals. Here, a court-assigned trustee will "administer" the estate of the debtor by selling non-legally protected (non-exempt) assets over a minimum amount, then using the money received to pay up the creditor. After the proceeds are divided by the creditors, the rest of the debt is forgiven. For a debtor with no non-exempt assets, which is usually the case, the bankruptcy is called a "no asset" case. After your account is discharged, creditors can no longer legally bother you again. Chapter 7 bankruptcy does not cover tax, tax-payment-incurred debt, student loans, child support, and alimony.

Note: Because of the new laws under the Bankruptcy Abuse Prevention and Consumer Protection Act of 2005, filing for Chapter 7 has become harder. The aim of the act is to:

I. Stop people from entering into bankruptcy if they are getting too much and are probably budgeting improperly—with bankruptcy stemming from excess credit card debts and quick cash personal loans.

II. Show consumers other ways of handling debt. For example, consumer credit counseling.

CHAPTER 11

Chapter 11 is called "rehabilitation" bankruptcy. Businesses and corporation use it to get more time for restructuring so as to ultimately pay their creditors. Individuals can use this chapter if they have debts assets and debts that are substantial, say over $922,000 in secured debts and over $307,000 in unsecured debts.

CHAPTER 13

Chapter 13 is a type of rehabilitation for individuals (with a regular income source) trying to keep their assets protected. In this case, you will agree to a repayment plan ordered by the court, which would last between three to five years. To qualify, some factors are considered, like your IRS consumer financial index. Failing to pay means you risk losing your assets.

If you are not qualified for Chapter 7, you may be able to use Chapter 13. With Chapter 13, you can keep your assets, but parts of your future income will be used in repaying creditors.

Hiring a Bankruptcy Attorney

Competent bankruptcy attorneys can be recommended through personal references or your state or county bar association. When meeting an attorney, come with physical documentation—a list of your creditors and accounts, copies of your collection letters and last statements (more may be later asked of you). Remember to ask beforehand your legal fees prior to the meeting.

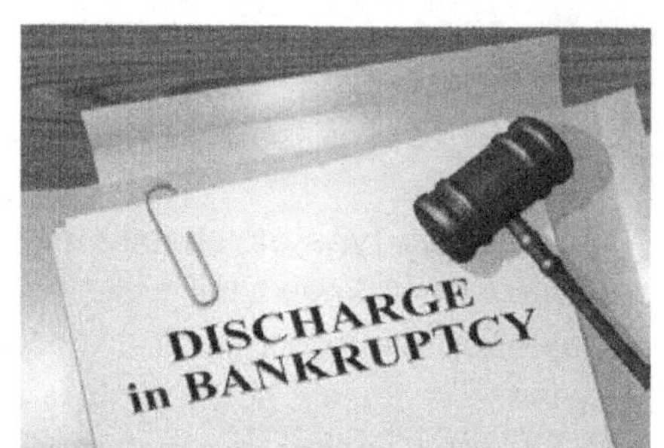

How Bankruptcy Affects Your Credit Report

When a bankruptcy case is completed, your updated credit report will show one of the following:

DISCHARGED

This is terrible news for unsecured creditors. A court-ordered "discharge" finalizes the bankruptcy and forgives Chapter 7-covered debts but reschedules Chapter 12-covered debts. Because debts like taxes, student loans, child support, and alimony are not forgiven, collection agencies might still come for you. A discharged bankruptcy can last up to a decade on your credit report.

DISMISSED

Because you do not qualify for bankruptcy protection, the court has dismissed your case, leaving you at the hands of collection authorities. A dismissed bankruptcy can stay up to seven years on your report.

WITHDRAWN

This is when, after filing, you no longer want bankruptcy protection. Your withdrawn bankruptcy can stay on your report for seven years.

If filing for a bankruptcy, just know that it can take up to 200 points off your credit score and its status can last up seven to ten years on your reports. Thankfully, as time goes by, your credit will begin to get better—and you will start getting credit offers in due time.

CHAPTER 12

Ten-Day Fix for Raising Your Credit Score: A Quick Fix for Mortgage Application

---

This Chapter Lectures About:

- Understanding The Rapid Re-Score Process
- How To Determine What's Really Affecting Your Scores
- How Assemble Your Information For Rapid Re-Scoring
- Repairing Techniques When Money Is An Issue
- Repairing Strategies That Require Money

If you are on the verge of applying for a mortgage and quickly need to raise your credit score (as much as 100 points) in about ten days, there are legal "hidden" maneuvers you can use by yourself.

Note that the results of your increase will only show in about 30-60 days.

In the mortgage industry, this method is called "rapid re-score." A re-score is presenting evidence of a changed data on your credit report to the CRAs and requesting an update to get a credit score recalculation. A mortgage or its third-party reseller (supplier of credit reports) usually provides this evidence to the CRAs.

All mortgage companies (e.g., lenders, brokers, bankers) can legally ask for a re-score. However, they have to pay a cost of $40 per item, per credit report. Because all three credit reports could be used, it may cost $120 to ask for a re-score of just a single item, like a credit card. Thankfully, you will likely pay the re-score fee as long as you agree with your creditor. It is not as simple as demanding a re-score. You need to show evidence of incorrect data that requires updating.

First, to raise your score, you have to tackle the significant factors affecting it first.

Knowing the Factors That Are Affecting Your Score

Most loan officers should be of assistance here since they depend on funded loans.

However, I know that a little "do it yourself" is possible. Your aim here is to raise your middle credit score, the median of all three credit reports. Say: If your TransUnion score is 499, Equifax score is 640, and Experian score is 585, then your middle score is 585. Even though your TransUnion report is below 500, most lenders will only make use of your median score.

Now you need to know why your score is low. Thanks to the FACT Act, you can see the factors affecting it when applying for a mortgage:

I. Excessive inquiries
II. Credit card balances
III. Late payments
IV. Collection accounts
V. Public records (e.g., tax liens, bankruptcy or civil judgment)

Note that because public records (tax liens and bankruptcies) cannot be tackled in a few days, only the four other score factors can be managed.

Assemble Your Evidence

To update your credit file, you need an acceptable evidence—a creditor-issued statement or letter. The letter should have the following requirements:

I. Dated within the past 30 days
II. Written on letterhead of creditor with contact information
III. Account holder's name and address
IV. Account number
V. A precise and plainly stated reference to what information is to be updated on the credit report (e.g. balance amount is $0)

VI. Signature from the creditor's representative

The CRAs will not accept:

I. Copies of canceled checks or money order receipts
II. Hand-written letters
III. Letters without contact information or a date
IV. Divorce decree
V. Paid receipts
VI. Third-party documentation

You have to be timely here so make sure your creditor faxes you this document. Come up with a believable sob story to hasten up the process if you have to.

▶▶ Quick Fixes without paying

Apart from paying for the re-score fee, there are several methods of avoiding further payments. But note that these methods do not guarantee a score raise. To raise your score without sending more cash, you can use:

▶▶ Excessive Inquiries

If you allegedly applied for a credit extension and your credit is pulled, your score drops by as much as five points. With five inquiries from different creditors on your file, you could lose up to 25 points. To boost your score, you have to sniff out unauthorized inquiries.

To do this, directly contact the companies that pulled your report and ask was the permissible purpose to pull your reports. You will need a letter from them stating that the inquiry was an error. Keep troubling them even when the inquiry is legitimately authorized.

▶▶ Credit Card Balances

Credit card balances take a significant portion credit score. A reported balance of $1 can affect your creditworthiness. However, because it takes up to 30, 60 or even 90 days for balances to be reported, and you know for sure that your credit card balance is much lower than the reported value on your report, contact your credit card company and request for a faxed letter attesting to your present-day balance. Doing this can help your score significantly.

►► Late Payments

Because a 30-day late payment on your account can significantly reduce your score, contact all creditors who have reported your late payments. It is true that you have the right to demand correction if you were never late. However, because you probably were, you can agree with your creditor—this is if you have a good and long prior relationship with each other and you have not been late more than twice.

First, contact the person in charge of the finance or credit reporting department. Through a faxed and personalized letter to this person, admit your error, plead for help concerning the removal of late payment and pledge your customer loyalty. Remember to draft an important-looking letter—with your professional title and letterhead.

While it is not a guaranteed method, it may work.

►► Collection Accounts

The only method of removing a collection account without first paying them off is prove to the current collection agency that the original creditor was paid. Medical collections are significant for this tactic if you can prove that your insurance paid the claim. To deal with collection agencies, you have to be firm but friendly. Even with considerable supporting evidence, you cannot just wait for your report to be traditionally updated after 30 or 60 days. You want to fax a letter attesting the payment quickly, so you have to come up with a convincing story.

Quick Fixes That Require Money

You can get a faster result when you spend a little. A little negotiating is not unlawful.

▶▶ Credit Card Balances

If the balances on your credit report are not zero, you have to pay up. However, if you do not have enough funds, you can appropriately allocate your payment:

First, clear off the smaller balances, then allocate the rest to the larger ones. Remember to make your payment overnight, using a local branch or over the internet or phone but void first class mail. As soon as your payment is made, go to the local branch and request an updated statement or a letter (from an assistant manager or an account representative) stating your account has a zero balance.

Do not let their company policy deny you an issued letter. Come up with a plausible sob story and keep pushing—but be friendly.

▶▶ Collection Agencies

It is not so simple here. It is not just about paying off the collection account; you also want the file deleted like it was never there. Of course, no collection account at all is better than a zero-balance collection account.

Now you have to arrange with the collection agency—promise to pay up a lump sum of your collection account in exchange for completely removing the negative information on your file. Most collection agency agencies will not talk about your request during a phone call. Just fax a letter to them. Do not worry—they want money too.

▶▶ Late Payments

Buying your way out of preceding late payments may not be possible. However, for your recent late payments, you can ask the creditor to re-age your account in exchange for paying a large portion of your outstanding balance. Here, you may start to hint bankruptcy to the creditor. Sadly, if you were late, to begin with, you may not have the money to pay now. However, if you can raise some cash, this tactic may work.

In the case of public records, you cannot touch them because of the time constraint. For a quick rise in your credit score, just put all your energy on your collection and creditors account.

When you get the documents needed from your creditors, have your loan officer submit them to the CRAs for a re-score—they will respond in three to five days. Note that it would take up to 30 to 60 days before your score is naturally updated.

CHAPTER 13

Managing Your Credit During A Marriage and Divorce

This Chapter Lectures About:

- The Conversations You Should Have Prior To Getting Married
- How To Handle Credit As Married Couple
- Strategizing For The Divorce – The Do's And Don'ts
- Notifying The Creditors and Safeguarding Yourself Through A Divorce

---

Your credit score is built solely on data. Your personal life, as well as your nationality, religion, race, gender or marital status does not affect your credit scores. Figuratively speaking, a divorce should not directly affect your score as well. However, due to the loss of a spouse, through demise or divorce, there is a high chance your score can ultimately be affected.

So, to stay ahead, you have to plan for these two situations:

Before Getting Married

Before marriage, have a sit-down with your loved one to assess both your current and future financial situations—this includes both of your credit reports. If you possess individual loans or credit accounts before tying the knot, try to keep them in your name. Avoid canceling them and do not add the name of your spouse to them—mainly when you are presently doing your best to keep them current. The fact is that when you lose a spouse, you may have to get a new home, insurance or job quickly, and this is where your credit score comes in. Moreover, amazingly, people with a lot of credit (even if some are bad ones) are placed higher than people with none.

By adding your spouse's name as a user to an existing account, you would be making him or her an authorized user.

While it is not a real joint account, your spouse will enjoy the benefits of the account like it was opened with both of your social security numbers.

To remove your spouse's name from your account, you have to make a few attempts.

Before getting married, plan how you and your spouse would manage credit issues. Start with your current credit situations. Assess both carefully and look for ways to maintain a good score and ways to avoid a bad one. A smart move is to stall your nuptials until both credit scores are good. Planning is key to good ratings—this is where a prenuptial or ante nuptial agreement comes in.

Prenuptial agreement is not just for preserving assets and limiting alimony. Credit issues also come into play, so planning how they would be managed during and at the end of the marriage matters a lot.

Your credit rating is an asset that needs protection. If a careless or spiteful spouse can misuse the asset of a good credit rating just like squandering a bank account, then you must include your credit into your prenuptial agreement.

If you are too romantic for a formal prenuptial agreement, try at least to plan your credit usage in a way that will be preserved as your asset. Fortunately, in the case of a divorce, a credit score is a non-marital asset that cannot be distributed. You always need to protect and care for it.

When you open joints accounts, you are intermingling your credit with your spouse's—note that this is very risky if his or her credit drops. However, if your spouse has a high score, you can leverage it by opening joint accounts. However, you still need simple maintenance and focus with regards to those accounts, because if finances take a downturn, so will your credit rating.

Creditors do not care about your marriage or divorce. If an account is joint, every party involved is responsible for it.

During the Marriage

From credit issues to debts, always get involved in your family's finances. A casual conversation about these issues can save you much time, legal fees and emotion. Especially when there is instability with their credit card account usage as well as poor payment patterns.

During the marriage, keep an eye on all your accounts: especially the ones you are linked to as either an authorized user (with signatory rights) or a joint account holder. Carefully monitor your mail and ask your husband or wife questions as their account statements arrive. Without offending your spouse, you can also go online and monitor each account, if they are reserved or secretive.

Note a red flag when your spouse is secretive about his or her finances; it is then you have to dig deeper and leverage for more information.

Before looking, wait. Do not just assume that your spouse is squandering a credit account on a secret lover or life. First, to be sure of your credit rating when looking, assess their non-payments, slow payments or increases in credit limits in your spouse's account. See if one credit card is being used to clear off others—this a sure sign of financial constraint. This action may not be malicious. He or she may have lost a job or entered into financial difficulty and thus embarrassed to talk about it.

Note that actions and inactions can make or break a marriage. Physical or mental incapacity during a marriage can cause financial worries and can shake the foundations of that relationship just like fiscal irresponsibility or infidelity. If you see something is being hidden from you or endangers your score, you can still protect your credit even in the worst-case scenario. Just do not worsen matters by acting tactlessly.

Planning for the Divorce

After deciding to end your marriage, quickly start planning for the divorce. Waiting brings no benefit. On the other hand, if you are unexpectedly served the divorce, your best action is to plan.

While they are many aspects to cover during a divorce (e.g., children), this chapter is dedicated to credit-related issues.

When planning your divorce, contact your attorney and a Certified Divorce Financial Planner (CDFP). The attorney's role is clear. The CDFP is simply a financial planner or an accountant who is solely specified in divorce-related financial issues. A CDFP will help you in planning your finances during pre and post-divorce times. If you have no earlier understanding the family finances, a CDFP can bring you up to date; if you already updated on your finances, a CDFP can help you better plan and organize your budgets and chose the right divisions.

Asset division during a divorce can be difficult when separating intangible and tangle debts and assets. For example, a common case where two significant assets, a retirement and a house have the same approximately the same value. Questions like "would you refinance?", "which should you pick?", "which should be split?" or "should you sell your house?" can best be answered with the help of a CDFP. While it feels evident that one spouse should take the retirement account while the other takes the house, it is never that simple. Questions of the house upkeep or the investment value of the two assets beyond their cash worth can best be answered by a proper professional.

Handling Your Accounts and Creditors

When planning your divorce, you must have a full understanding of every credit account opened as a family as well the names the accounts are held. If you are an authorized user (with signature privileges), the creditor sees you as a liable debtor, so it is more or less like a joint account. The best move is close every joint account; for accounts in your name, remove the other spouse's name, to remove the chances of them incurring additional debt that you may be liable for. From the point when you decide on divorce to when you actually file the paperwork, your credit stays in a crucial period, because a spouse can accumulate debt, knowing the end is near. With your joint accounts, the spouse may buy more cars, new clothes and pay for legal fees. When you plan well, you can prevent this scenario.

One crucial step is to quickly pull your credit report when you have internally decided on a divorce and also pull up it before the divorce is finalized. If everything appears as it should, your report should clearly state the conditions of each account: whether you are an authorized user of the accounts, whether they jointly held with your ex, or whether they held by solely by you. Your report will not show if there is an authorized user on your accounts. If you are not very sure, call each creditor and say you no longer authorize any other users (especially your ex) on that account; remember to back it up with a letter.

In case of a loan account, or when the creditor declines to close an account with a balance, ask the creditor to "freeze" the account. For a "frozen" account, no party can raise the debt on it or charge it. Sadly, you cannot stop another party from re-opening a previous or existing account. Just keep your requests to the creditor in writing and always review your credit reports every six months.

According to a general rule, which creditors follow, every debt sustained during the marriage, no matter the circumstance, is a marital liability—meaning the spouses are both liable. To deal with joint debts, a good move may involve one spouse paying off the debt alone. A better move is using the marital assets to pay it off. The best move would be to close the account (when absolutely paid off), so there is no chance of it incurring more debt.

However, for a joint credit card account, your ex can still charge on it. Moreover, if there is a way to divide up the debt, there is a chance your ex will not make timely payments. Be sure your divorce decree permits you to file a reimbursement lawsuit against your ex if you are ever forced to make that account current. Know that the court cannot order the CRAs to delete the negative information on your reports. Another move is to seek the advice of your attorney about agreeing to take over some specific loan and credit card accounts in exchange for a larger property settlement. In this case, you will personally see to the timely payment of the debt and not depend on your ex.

If there is an immense debt, and there are assets available, perhaps a home, it is smart to sell the assets to pay off and close joint debts. Forget the emotional attachment and embrace the change. It will benefit both parties in the long run.

During and after a divorce, a realistic budget is needed to stay afloat, because you do not know what is coming to your way post-divorce, in child support or alimony. The divorce process should not affect your creditworthiness. Budget the amount that would be incurred during the process. To avoid bad credit, it is smarter to sell your house to pay off large debts, instead of struggling to maintain a home that is eating off large portions of your income.

The right outcome during a divorce is separating all of your financial obligations, instead of keeping joint assets or debt and trying to manage them together after the divorce. However, if a judge is needed to make a ruling on this, you may face this latter outcome, and it will not benefit you. The smart settlement is always out of court and among yourselves. Be sure to enter a "marital settlement agreement" where every issue is clearly and correctly spelled out.

According to your state law and your attorney's draft, your settlement agreement can be as detailed as possible. It should clearly state every detail about splitting up or paying up your debt. However, in reality, lenders and credit card companies do not care about your divorce arrangements or what the judge's order.

If your divorce decree or agreement states that your spouse is to be legally responsible for a specific debt, creditors can still come for you when that spouse defaults. So if your social security number or name was used to open a credit card or loan, or you are registered as an authorized user, "turning over" that account to your ex may not stop your credit report from being negatively affected if that ex-spouse does not pay up promptly.

For personal loans, secured debt (e.g., car loans), mortgages, splitting up the debt is the right move. But you will have to re-finance or liquidate all of it so that your ex-spouse's name is no longer connected to the ownership of the debt.

The cold fact of a post-divorce is that, before some financial arrangement can be finalized, both parties may need to get back their feet: for example, when a mortgage has to be re-financed for the sake of both parties if you cannot put your home on sale presently, state in writing that it will be sold before a specific date or upon an eventuality, like when all the kids reach the age of 18.

It is hard to say, but it is the truth: do not let emotions cloud your minds during a divorce. You must be able to account for every financial aspect of the marriage because missing out one item (perhaps a credit card opened years ago by your ex) can come back and get you in many years to come.

CHAPTER 14

When a Creditor Sues You

This Chapter Lectures About:

- Understanding How Lawsuits Work
- You Have Been Served – What's Next
- What Should Be Researched Before You React
- The Types Of Court When Being Sue By A Creditor
- Attorney Fees And How They Are Collected

To collect their money when you are late on payments or have defaulted your bills, collection agencies or creditors may file a lawsuit against you. Your next move is to quickly contact your attorney because it is imperative that you provide a legal response to the suit within a couple of days.

How a Lawsuit Works

The party who files the suit, whether a collection agency or creditor, is called the (e.g., a creditor/collection agency) is known as the Plaintiff, Petitioner or Complainant. The party that is being sued, the alleged debtor or consumer, is known as the Respondent or Defendant.

A lawsuit consists of three parts:

▶▶ Summons

This is the first document received by a Defendant-debtor from the Plaintiff (the creditor). This document provides a Defendant with necessary information like the Plaintiff's name and address as well as the address of the court where the case has been taken. This document also states either the time period within which the Defendant must respond to the Complaint or a scheduled time or date the Defendant and Plaintiff must make an appearance in court.

▶▶ Complaint

A Complaint is the Plaintiff's (creditor's) side of the story; it consists of a detailed account of why the Plaintiff should win the case and the entitled damages.

▶▶ Service of Process

The Service of Process is a kind of receipt that shows that the Summons and Complaint were delivered at a particular date, to activate the deadlines shown in the Summons.

According to most state statutes,

once the Summons and Complaint are submitted with the courts, they must be served upon the Defendant within 90 to 120 days. In case of an improper serving of the Summons and Complaint within that time frame, the Plaintiff must pay a new fee and may be asked to re-file.

The Various Types Service of Process

Several factors, like your alleged debt and state of residence, can determine how you would be served. The usual ways are:

SHERIFF

A sheriff comes to your home with the documents. If you are not at home, he or she can leave with a member of your household member above a particular age.

PROCESS SERVER

A process server is just like a private investigator hired to find you wherever you are.

POSTAL CARRIER

Via a postal carrier, lawsuit documents can also be mail-delivered.

"Hiding" from a being served is of no use. If the servers cannot find you, the court will be on the side of the Plaintiff. While the court may ask the Plaintiff to make more efforts to notify you, e.g., publish a notice in the local newspapers, if the Plaintiff can prove to have made all reasonable attempts and show that you are intentionally avoiding service, the case will go on without you, and you will lose in a default judgment.

So, when you find out that you are about to be served, quickly accept it.

Your First Move

Even when you have maintained excellent communication with your creditors, do not be shocked by the lawsuit. Of course, the creditors can lawfully do this when you do not pay on time.

But even when a law firm or collection agency sends you a prior letter warning a lawsuit, you still cannot know which creditor will sue you. You can be sued for an account with a comparatively small balance in contrast to larger (perhaps defaulted) accounts. To wiggle out of all these lawsuits, you need the advice of an experienced attorney.

There is even a possible chance that you may have been sued and were not unaware of it. If you discover a judgment or lawsuit on your report, quickly find out more about the case. If it is a locally filled case, visit the courthouse and request for a copy of the case from the clerk's office or go online to the local clerk of courts department and search the creditor's name or your name.

After finding the case, review all associated documents to the lawsuit, either the clerk's office or through the courthouse computer. The information of the Plaintiff, consisting of the name and number of the attorney filing the case, must be on these lawsuit documents.

If you are sure that you were not served properly, you can try to dispute via the court system that the service was defective. Of course, you need the advice of an attorney to do this. Just showing up before the final hearing to complain to the judge about the service will only prove that you are already aware of the proceedings and thus be reflected in the court file.

While the process of a lawsuit is the same in most states, you must be knowledgeable about your responsibilities and right according to your local and state laws.

TIP: A letter sent by the creditor's lawyer does not mean that you will be sued; it could be a scare tactic to pay up. However, when faced with a real lawsuit, stay calm. You will gain nothing from worrying. Next, read the received documents carefully. Because these documents might be written in legal mumbo-jumbo, it is best you quickly find an attorney. If you cannot afford one, ask the court for assistance.

Even after hiring a lawyer, try to understand the basics of the case against you. Most times, two original copies of the same document are delivered to you. Carefully read them to be sure that they are the same—not for two separate accounts. Be sure to keep one copy for yourself.

The fact is that if you are in default or delinquent with one loan or credit card, you are probably having the same issues with others, too. Creditors nationwide have the law firms in your area (especially those specializing in collection law) on retainer. So, it is possible to receive different lawsuits from two more different creditors through just a single law firm. If you get several papers, remember to read them carefully.

Even when you leave the originals with your lawyer, be sure to make one extra copy for each document you receive. You can choose to leave everything to your lawyer, but it is essential for you to understand the basic parts of your lawsuit.

You also need to carefully read the pages to see if any of your assets or bank accounts are listed on it. In cases like this, it shows that someone is performing an asset search to frighten you into the thought of forfeiting your assets.

This is usually found as an attachment to the lawsuit—called "A Writ of Attachment." This document—used by the creditor to invoke the General Attachment Statute—provides a list of all your bank accounts and owned real asset. If your state is among the few (New Hampshire, Massachusetts, and Connecticut) under the statute, the creditor can use it to prevent any transfer of your property. To release your property, in this case, you will have to post a bond as security for any judgment awarded to the Plaintiff-Creditor.

The Types of Court

When being sued by a creditor, the case either falls into:

1. CIVIL COURT: a full litigation experience with judges, lawyers, witnesses and juries
2. SMALL CLAIMS COURT: a simple forum for consumers without a lawyer.

Civil Courts are for serious cases where there is the need for a judge or/and jury. Examples of such cases are child custody rights, alimony issues, criminal and felony cases—cases with jail times and hefty fines as well as cases that involve repaying a debt of more than $15,000.

Small Claims Court is a state court that deals with non-criminal cases by protecting private rights or recovering financial damages for wrongs suffered or "smaller amount" money owed. Cases here included unpaid bills claims, property damage claims, personal injury, land/tenant disputes—all which alleged debt do not go beyond a specific amount.

Your response to a lawsuit should be "subject to" if the case is filed in a Civil Court or Small Claims Court. For Small Claims matters, the court document gives a set of instructions for you. You are usually asked to attend a court hearing known as Pre-Trial Hearing or Pre-Trial Conference at an arranged date and time. The courtroom is filled with consumers in similar cases; then each consumer is called to the bench one case at a time.

Next, the judge will request a brief explanation of the case. A summary of the case is first brought forward by the Plaintiff's lawyer. Then, the judge will request for your version of the story. Note this is not an official argument; it is just a way for the judge to begin to comprehend the situation.

The judge will probably ask both parties whether they will settle between themselves or come to an agreement. If you do not agree to the settlement plan put forward by the Plaintiff, the judge might then direct both parties to an independent third-party mediator who will "help" the judge in helping both parties come to a satisfactory resolution.

Attorneys' Fees

Attorney's fees can be in:

FLAT FEE

A flat fee covers the whole representation for a specific issue. If the fee is substantial, you can be asked to pay in installments.

HOURLY FEE

An hourly fee is a specified amount paid to a lawyer for each hour of work done. In this case, an upfront non-refundable payment may be asked by the lawyer before any work can be done.

CONTINGENCY

A contingency fee is based on the financial outcome of a case. If you are the Plaintiff and win the case, a percentage of the awarded damaged (30 percent to 40 percent) is given to the lawyer. Because Defendants usually do not get any monetary rewards, this arrangement does not apply to them.

CHAPTER 15

Establishing or Re-Establishing Credit

This Chapter Lectures About:

- The Facts Behind How To Obtain Gas Cards
- Using Banking Relationships To Build Credit
- When You Should Apply For A Secured Card
- Using A Co-Signer To Help Build Scores
- Ways To Get Added To Authorized User Accounts
- Quick Recap Of Maintaining A Good Credit Score

No matter what your credit situation is, you can still establish or re-establish your creditworthiness. However, to achieve this, you must have done everything necessary to delete the adverse items from your credit file. Alternatively, a premature application for new credit can worsen your rating due to excessive inquiries.

You do not have to delete all negative items: follow the preliminary instructions in this book.

Gasoline and Department Store Cards

Because these types of cards have comparatively smaller credit limits and these companies want you to purchase their products, make these cards easier to get approved for. Moreover, since charging is only possible at their stores and stations, companies benefit from these cards. Most times, approval is done quickly at the checkout counter—even without your personal information being verified. With just marginal credit, approval is possible. When applying for a gasoline card, be sure it is not co-branded with a MasterCard or VISA logo because these have stricter approval requirements than the ones used solely for gasoline and food purchases.

Neighborhood Banker

Just like major banks nationwide, in other to build a relationship with you, local banks and credit unions can provide a small line of credit. Even with poor credit, they may relax their scoring rules in return for security (a secured savings account or certificate of deposit) to certify your timely payments. So, when you pay off the loan, you will be granted further loans or a larger credit limit. Just get in touch with them.

Secured Credit Cards

Secured credit cards function just like unsecured cards; however, they are designed for people with poor credit ratings.

Caution: From stringent penalty fees for late payments to stiff annual fees to high-interest rates, maintenance of secured credit cards is highly expensive. Consider not using your secured card for regularly spending. Just use this account as a tool to establish your credit. Alternatively, you may worsen your credit situation when the limits and fees surpass your means.

In the case of secured cards, the bank or finance company lets you open a certificate of deposit (CD) for an equal amount to the credit line given to you (usually a few hundred dollars). So, for example, in opening a CD with $300, $300 (minus the initial or application fees) will probably be your credit line. To enjoy the benefits of the account, be sure that the credit card company reports to the three major CRAs.

Note that prepaid cards do not report to the CRAs.

One or two years after re-establishing your credit, you can ask the creditor whether they are willing to change the secured account into a non-secured one. No matter what, never close a secured account until you have converted it into an unsecured one. Or else, you will have to possess the self-control of not using it.

In keeping a zero balance, your credit score will significantly rise. Remember to never go beyond five credit cards. To underwrite a loan, mortgage lenders providing the best interest rates require at least three open accounts on your credit file. So, with five accounts, you should meet the requirements. Always maintain a low balance and make timely payments.

Use a Co-Signer

In your best interest, it is not recommended to act as "co-signer" for another person. However, if someone can act as one for you, then you are in luck. If you have a co-signer with excellent credit, you will get loans and card approval quickly. While you may not risk being a co-signer, others might not as well. Do not break a relationship to become creditworthy. Only use a co-signer when it is essential, like when financing your vehicle.

Become an Authorized User

This is just like co-signing; however, there is no application process involved. It is all about having your spouse, family member or friend add you to their credit card account to get a quick credit boost. The primary account holder risks a lot in granting you the authority to sign on his or her account. However, to free yourself from this hassle, tell your family and friend that you do not require your own card; you need their account history on your credit report. So if they keep making timely payments, you are good. If they start defaulting, your credit will be affected as well. Thankfully, at any point in time, you or the primary holder of the account could demand your removal as an authorized user.

Maintain Your Credit

To maintain your credit after establishing or re-establishing it, you must:

▶▶ Pay Your Bills on Time

Timely payment of monthly bills should be obvious. Still, you should be paying attention to the grace period for each credit card or loan. Doing this saves your credit score and also saves you from incurring extra charges.

▶▶ Monitor Your Credit Report

Once a year, you can pull up your report for free or choose to pay for more copies. If you can prove to the CRAs that you have an issue, you can get many copies for free. However, never wait around if you sense a problem. Get it right away for a minimal fee.

▶▶ Balance Transfers: Read Carefully

By reading your agreements, you will discover several things. Especially when you are being pushed to transfer your balance to another company because of its lower interest rates, carefully read the agreement. The low-interest rate may only last for a short duration or may only cover the transferred balances. Showing longtime loyalty to your original credit card company has several benefits and can even improve your credit report. In return for your loyalty after showing your worthiness (with timely payments), you can ask your current creditors for better deals and lower interest rates.

▶▶ Control Your Credit Card Use

Consider limiting the usage of your credit cards. Do not use them daily! That is the job of a debit card. Your credit cards should be used on special occasions or emergencies, such as vacations, car repairs, and medical procedures.

▶▶ Using Credit Freeze or Fraud Alert

In the case of identity theft, the CRAs have designed free extra levels of protection for your reports.

A "fraud alert" is a note on your credit file that states that you are a fraud victim (or think so). So, in case of a identify theft during a credit application, before the creditor submits that application, he or she is instructed to call you directly beforehand for confirmation.

A credit "freeze" provides another level of protection which stops anyone from opening your account even with your information. When you "freeze" the account, even you cannot open your account. Note that a fraud alert or credit freeze can also be used in case of a malicious ex or a bad divorce.

CONSUMER PROTECTION LAWS TIMELINES

Our federal government plays an important role in the credit consumer rights process. Although they take no part in scoring, the Federal Trade Commission is tasked with upholding your consumer rights, preventing companies and individuals from causing you unfair harm. It wasn't always easy to assert credit rights and repair past mistakes. However, years of progress has led to the following legislation decision:

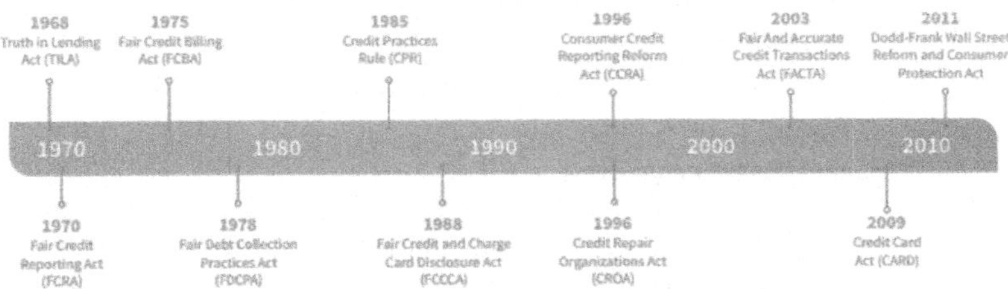

- **1968: Truth in Lending Act (TILA)**—When providing a contract, credit companies must list their terms, conditions and costs to customers.
- **1970: Fair Credit Reporting Act (FCRA)**—As an amendment to the Consumer Credit Protection Act, the FCRA requires banks to maintain records and report transactions to the Department of the Treasury. It also allows you to check your credit reports, verify and maintain your information. This law is the cornerstone of credit repair.
- **1975: Fair Credit Billing Act (FCBA)**—As an amendment to the Truth in Lending Act, the FCBA protects consumers from unfair billing practices, allowing you to combat and dispute errors.

- **1978: Fair Debt Collection Practices Act (FDCPA)**—As an amendment to the Consumer Credit Protection Act, the FDCPA limits how creditors can contact you to collect debts.

- **1985: Credit Practices Rule (CPR)**—This law limits the types of creditor requirements listed in contracts. It also requires them to list your borrower responsibilities in writing before asking you to sign an agreement.

- **1988: Fair Credit and Charge Card Disclosure Act (FCCCA)**—As part of TILA, credit providers must list the following information on their card applications:

    - Percent APR
    - Minimum finance charges
    - Grace period on purchases
    - Balance calculation methodology
    - Annual fees
    - Transaction fees on cash advances
    - Penalty fees for late payments and overspending without overdraft coverage

- **1996: Consumer Credit Reporting Reform Act (CCRA)**—As an amendment to the FCRA, this law provides the following people with free credit reports:

    - Unemployed
    - Those on public-assistance
    - Fraud/identity theft victims
    - Every consumer (on an annual basis)

- **1996: Credit Repair Organizations Act (CROA)**—This law regulates how creditors may advertise their products, allowing consumers to make an informed decision.

- **2003: Fair And Accurate Credit Transactions Act (FACTA)**—As an extension to the FCCCA, this law limits how credit reports are used.

- **2009: Credit Card Act (CARD)**—This law limits how much and how often creditors may raise interest rates, impose fees, allocate payments, and most importantly, market and provide new credit to college students.

- **2011: Dodd-Frank Wall Street Reform and Consumer Protection Act**—This law created the Bureau Of Consumer Financial Protection which regulates how creditors and bankers treat consumers.

CREDIT REPORTING ACRONYMS

- **CRA** – A CRA is a commonly used acronym for a credit reporting agency. Equifax, Experian and TransUnion are the generally recognized credit reporting agencies, although there are several more.
- **FCRA** – The FCRA is the Fair Credit Reporting Act which, among other things, defines your rights vis-à-vis free annual credit reports and getting errors corrected.
- **CDIA** – The CDIA is the Consumer Data Industry Association, which is the trade association of the credit reporting industry.
- **VSS** – VSS is VantageScore Solutions, which is the company that maintains the VantageScore credit scoring system.
- **FICO** – FICO is Fair Isaac Corporation, which is the company that maintains the FICO credit scoring system.
- **FCBA** – The Fair Credit Billing Act is the Federal statute that limits our liability on credit card fraud to no more than $50.
- **EFTA** – The Electronic Funds Transfer Act is the Federal statute that limits our liability on debit card fraud to no more than $500.
- **FDCPA** – The Fair Debt Collection Practices Act defines how 3rd party debt collection companies have to operate re: collecting delinquent debts from consumers.
- **CROA** – The Credit Repair Organizations Act is the Federal statute that defines how credit repair companies have to operate when offering credit improvement services to consumers
- **ACDV** – An Automated Credit Dispute Verification form is used by the credit reporting agencies to communicate consumer disputes to lenders and collection agencies. The non-automated predecessor to the ACDV was the CDV, which stands for Consumer Dispute Verification form

- **AUD** - An Automated Universal Data form is used by lenders and collection agencies to proactively correct or modify information on a consumer's credit reports. The non-automated predecessor to the AUD was the UDF, which stands for Universal Data Form.
- **CRO** - A Credit Repair Organization is a company, as defined by Federal and state law, that markets and sells credit report improvement services to consumers for a fee.
- **e-OSCAR** - Online Solution for Complete and Accurate Reporting is the communication protocol used by the credit reporting agencies to communicate disputes to their furnishing companies, normally a lender or a collection agency.
- **PACER** - Public Access to Court Electronic Records is used by the credit reporting agencies to collect bankruptcy information, which is then placed on consumer credit reports.
- **AA Letter** - An AA letter is an "Adverse Action" letter, which is a declination letter. If you are denied credit because of your credit report and/or credit score the lender is obligated by Federal law to send you an Adverse Action letter.

Glossary of Credit Card Terms

Below is a list of credit card and credit industry terms which can assist with reading credit card statements as well as the fine print on credit related documents.

- **Adjusted Balance** - The issuer calculates a balance by subtracting payments or credits received during the current billing period from the balance at the end of the previous billing period.
- **Affinity Card** - A co-marketed credit card that typically offers some type of incentive like rewards for cardholder loyalty. Both the issuer and brand associated with the card benefit financially from card use.
- **Annual Fee** - The amount charged or fee for use of a credit card product for a calendar year.
- **Annual Percentage Rate (APR)** - Acronym for: Annual Percentage Rate. This is the interest rate that a customer is charged on any outstanding balance over a given calendar year.
- **Application** - A form used for filling out personal credit information when applying for new credit. An application to a credit card issuer and subsequent approval is based on credit worthiness.
- **Application Fee** - A fee associated with processing a credit card application. These are highly uncommon and should raise red flags with applicants who are requested to pay one.
- **Approval Response** - This is the response period of time for a merchant when approving a transaction.
- **APR** - Acronym for Annual Percentage Rate.
- **Authorized Amount** - Within credit card transactions, this is the approved amount to be charged for a transaction and is deducted from the available open amount of credit.

- **Authorized User** - This is someone who is connected with a credit card account and can charge freely. However, an authorized user is not the main account holder and isn't responsible for payment of charges incurred on the account.
- **Auto-draft** - A program with a bank or credit card provider that automatically takes money from an account. This is also referred to as "auto-debit", and it is mostly used to pay recurring bills every month.
- **Available Credit** - This is the amount of credit or money available for charge to an individual card account holder.
- **Average Daily Balance** - A formula used by credit card issuers to determine the amount of interest charged over a given period of time (e.g. Month).
- **Bad Credit** - A term used to describe an individual's credit worthiness. Typically, an individual with a credit score of less than 620 would be considered a higher than normal credit risk and therefore, possessing bad credit.
- **Balance** - A balance is the remaining amount owed after all payments or credits to a given financial institution for charges on the account.
- **Balance Chasing** - A method used by some banks to lower available credit to account holders in an effort to curb spending and force them to pay down outstanding balances.
- **Balance Transfer** - The movement of a credit card balance from one credit card to another credit card.
- **Balance Transfer Fee** - The fee charged by a credit card issuer for transferring one balance from a credit card to another credit card. Typically a percentage of the total balance amount and is assessed each transfer.
- **Balance-to-limit Ratio** - This ratio calculates the amount of outstanding credit available to an individual or business against the amount of credit used or current outstanding balances. The lower the ratio, typically, the lower of a credit risk.

- **Bank** - A financial institution that is in the business of providing credit and other financial services.
- **Bank Holding Company** - A company or firm which holds a majority control in one or more US banking entities. Each credit card issuer has a parent bank holding company which oversees their operations. Bank holding companies are supervised by the Federal Reserve Board.
- **Basis Point** - One hundredth of one percentage point. If an interest rate increases by 2.0%, this equates to 200 basis points.
- **Billing Cycle** - The length of time between billing statement dates.
- **Billing Statement** - An official notice or statement which outlines all transactions, payments, interest charged and fees for a given individual or business account. This is sent by mail or e-mail depending the account holder's preference. Also referred to as a Periodic Statement.
- **Card Issuer** - Any financial entity that issues credit cards to card holders.
- **Card Member** - Also referred to as an account holder. This individual or business entity is authorized to use a credit card.
- **Card Member Agreement** - The card member agreement is a binding agreement which outlines the terms and conditions of a card holder's account. Federal law requires financial institutions to disclose all related financial formulas for using a credit card as well as resolution practices.
- **Cash Advance** - Cash advances from a credit card are considered a direct loan. Different rates and fees apply versus a card holder's regular APR. These tend to have very high interest rates and can result in significant interest amounts very quickly.
- **Cash Advance Check** - A check which is used to receive a cash loan against the available credit on a credit card. Sometimes these are referred to as convenience checks.
- **Cash Advance Fee** - A fee associated with requesting cash from the available credit of a credit card. Typically, these cost $50 to $75 and aren't connected with a percentage amount fee.

- **Cash Advance Rate** - The interest rate charged on the cash received from a cash advance on a credit card. Typically, these rates are double the purchase or balance transfer interest rate.
- **Cash Card** - Cash cards contain funds already placed in an account which is not tied to an individual banking account and can be withdrawn from ATMs. They can also be used to make purchases at retailers.
- **Charge Back** - A charge back is a returned transaction from the receiving bank back to the merchant. Charge backs are typically related to purchase disputes in which a bank customer doesn't recognize a charge or is disputing it with a merchant.
- **Charge Card** - A charge card requires that the full outstanding balance be paid after each billing cycle. Contrary to credit cards, charge card balances cannot be paid over time.
- **Charge Off** - The value of non-collectable credit card balances which are applied to a bank's loss reserves. Most credit card companies seek collection of past due accounts for up to 6 months.
- **Charge Off Rate** - The percentage of total outstanding credit card balances which have been deemed as non-collectable by the issuing firm.
- **Chip and Pin Cards** - A smart card which uses computer chips to collect and submit information versus the industry standard magnetic strip.
- **Closed Loop** - A gift or credit card which can only be used in a select or grouping of specific locations.
- **Co-Signer** - An additional person who agrees to be liable for any outstanding loan if it cannot be serviced by the main signer on the account.
- **Co-Branded Card** - A dual marketed credit card by a bank and consumer brand. Examples include airline mile credit cards or department store credit cards.

- **Concierge Service** - An extra customer service benefit intended to assist with hospitality services such as travel arrangements, dinner reservations and tickets to a local show.

- **Consumer Credit File** - A consolidated report which contains an individual's existing credit accounts, payment history and whether or not they have filed for bankruptcy or have existing liens against them. Consumer Credit Report Referred to by the Federal Reserve as a G.19 report. A credit report is the common term used to describe the official credit history of an individual with a valid social security number. Credit Reports are updated monthly by credit bureaus such as TransUnion, Experian and Equifax.

- **Convenience Checks** - Checks which can be drawn against an individual's available credit line. Convenience checks are typically considered cash advances and hold higher interest rates than standard credit card rates.

- **Credit Bureau** - A company which collects credit information to be accessed by companies to assist lenders with gauging an individual's credit risk.

- **Credit Bureau Risk Score** - A score assigned to an individual's credit history to evaluate their credit worthiness versus the rest of the population.

- **Credit Card** - A form of payment accepted by merchants during the point of sale to process payment for goods and / or services. Credit card holders may have the option to pay merchant balances over time.

- **Credit Card Act 2009** - Credit Card Accountability, Responsibility and Disclosure Act of 2009 Also known as the Credit CARD Act of 2009, this act instated a requirement on existing credit card owners to give advanced notice on important changes on credit card terms at least 45 days in advance which gives consumers 21 days for paying bills. The law was signed in May 2009, but took until February 22, 2010 to be fully instated.

- **Credit Card Number** - A series of digits that connects the owner with his/her card. The first six numbers relate the card to the issuer identification number (Visa, American Express, etc) The left over numbers are original to each card. The digits are imprinted onto the cards for machines that take imprints of cards instead of swiping them.

- **Credit Counselor** - The purpose of a credit counselor is to help customers escape debt by encouraging a debt management plan organized by creditors. Consumers are recommended to stay with credit counselors who are associated with nationally recognized agencies by financial experts.

- **Credit Freeze** - A credit freeze is an option consumers have to lock their credit making it impossible to open new accounts. It is commonly used when identity theft has occurred or is thought to have occurred. Fees are usually incurred for credit freezes unless proof of identity theft is available. There is also a charge when a consumer decides to reactivate the account or "thaw" the account.

- **Credit History** - Credit History is a record of an individual's past borrowing and repaying of money. It is managed by three main credit bureaus: Experian, TransUnion, and Equifax. The information is brought together to create a credit report. The report is used by credit card companies in deciding whether or not to issue an individual with credit and how much. The Fair Credit Reporting Act is responsible for keeping the information on consumer's credit reports.

- **Credit Inquiry** - Credit inquiry begins when a consumer is applying for a loan of some sort. A particular lender can research the credit history of the potential client by checking his/her credit report. Every time there is a credit inquiry it is documented and multiple inquiries can report negatively on the individual's credit scores. For more information see soft inquiry and hard inquiry.

- **Credit Life Insurance** - A policy designed to insure the balance of the primary cardholder is repaid in the case of death. This insurance can be purchased upon being issued credit by the primary cardholder.

- **Credit Limit** - The credit limit is the maximum amount of money that can be spent on a credit card. The credit limit on a card can be negatively or positively influenced by the credit scores. Minimum borrowing on credit leads to a higher credit score.

- **Credit Line** - A credit line is how much money can be put onto a credit account. The credit line is largely influenced by the consumers credit score. A good credit report leads to a higher credit line.
- **Credit Monitoring Service** - A credit monitoring service is one that watches the activity of the credit card holder. If unnatural or out of character charges occur, the service notifies the card holder. This service is usually billed to the consumer monthly or annually.
- **Credit Obligation** - A credit obligation is a legally binding contract that a consumer signs upon borrowing money that says the loan will be paid back. An example of a credit obligation is an installment loan such as a loan for a car.
- **Credit Rating** - Credit rating is a calculation of the past behavior of a borrower. It is a combination of income, employment, and history of repayment and is a way for a potential loaner to have an idea of the likelihood of repayment.
- **Credit Report** - A credit report is a collection of information on the history of a credit holder. It is a combination of credit inquiries, borrowing history, and the payment behavior of the individual. They are derived from complicated formulas that are used by possible lenders in determining the credit worthiness of a possible client.
- **Credit Reporting Agency** - There are three main agencies, Experian, Equifax, and TransUnion and they are responsible for organizing and reporting information about an individual. They use the payment behavior to create a credit report.
- **Credit Score** - A credit score is a numerical combination of three numbers that are compiled from formulas using a person's credit history and how timely they paid off their debt. The lower the number the more likely an individual is to be turned down for a loan. The higher the score the more likely an individual or a business is to receive better rates on a loan. FICO is known for its use of credit scores and its formula for credit score is the most often used.
- **Credit Union** - A credit union is a group of people that can compile their assets and provide credit cards to an individual or business.

The group of people usually has a bond by concentration, location or employment.

- **Credit Utilization Ratio** - Credit utilization ratio is a comparison of an individual's credit card balance and the credit limits. The lower the ratio the better, meaning that there is little debt but a good deal of credit is helpful for a credit score.
- **Currency Conversion Fee** - A currency conversion fee is also known as a foreign transaction fee. It a charge on a credit card when it is used in a foreign country in a foreign bank.
- **Debit** - Debits are, in terms of consumers, a charge put onto an account. When an individual has a checking or savings account, he or she can use a debit card to take money out a particular account in the bank. They can be created by writing a check, using an ATM or purchasing something from a merchant.
- **Debit Card** - A debit card is different from a credit card. A debit card is used to take money from a particular account. The money is already there whereas a credit card is used to create a loan. The credit card bill is paid at a later point. In order to use a debit card, an individual is asked to punch in a PIN or signing.
- **Debt Consolidation** - Debt consolidation is a way to centralize your debt in order to lower your monthly payments and interest rate.
- **Debt-to-Income Ratio** - Debt to income ratio is a personal measure of the amount of money you earn (gross income) to the percentage that is paid towards debt. This comes into play when applying for a mortgage. The higher the debt being paid off, the more likely it is for an individual to pay a higher rate for his/her mortgage.
- **Debt-to-limit Ratio** - The debt-to-limit ratio is a comparison of an individual's credit card balance and the credit limits. The lower the ratio the better, meaning that there is little debt but a good deal of credit, is helpful for a credit score.
- **Default APR** - A default APR(annual percentage rate) is an interest rate that can be applied to your credit card payment if you are late making a payment. It is also called a penalty rate.

- **Default Rate** - A default rate is an interest rate that is very high. It usually occurs when an individual is late making a payment or a card holder does not follow the terms and conditions on the card. It is also called a penalty rate.
- **Deferred Interest** - Deferred interest is usually advertised on car commercials saying "pay no interest until..." It is a payment plan that offers to postpone interest until a certain date. Once that date hits though, the interest that has been accruing is added to the account.
- **Deleveraging** - Deleveraging is an attempt to lower the financial leverage that is in place. It is done by paying off loans or debt.
- **Delinquent Account** - A delinquent account is one that is past due but in the case of a credit card holder, it is usually not reported unless it is past 30 days overdue. For example, in a student account at a university, if the payment is not received by the due date it is considered a delinquent account and is subject to a monthly penalty fee.
- **Discount Rate** - A discount rate is a charge, usually between 1 and 3 percent, that merchants must pay to credit card companies in order to use generally accepted credit cards.
- **Dormancy fee** - This fee was imposed on credit card accounts that had not been used in a long time or were dormant. If an account was considered inactive, the card company would apply the fee to the account to boost their income. It was popular in 2009 and part of 2010, but was banned when the final rules for the law came out. It is also known as inactivity fees.
- **Dormant Account** - A dormant account is one of inactivity or no use at all. In some cases, if a certain amount of time has passed of inactivity, credit card issuers will close the account. It is also known as an inactive account.
- **Double-cycle billing** - Double-cycle bulling a way to calculate how much interest must be paid on balances left on credit cards from month to month. It considers the current balance on the credit card and the average daily balance from the previous billing period. It was banned by the Credit CARD Act of 2009. It is also known as two-cycle billing.

- **Due Date** - A due date is when a credit card bill is required to be paid by. If the bill does not arrive, or has not been posted by the date it is due, a late fee will be imposed. Some companies allow their customers to set their own due dates so as to avoid late payments.

- **Electronic Funds Transfer Act** - The Electronic Funds Transfer Act is federal legislation that determines what is appropriate and inappropriate for customers who transfer their funds electronically. It was passed in 1978 by US Congress to establish the rights and liabilities of the customers.

- **Encryption** - An encryption is a way to securely transport credit card information across the internet or credit card processing networks. It is a code on the card that keeps it secured.

- **Equal Credit Opportunity Act** - The Equal Credit Opportunity Act is a US law enacted in 1974 that makes it impossible for a creditor to discriminate in lending against any applicant. it allows consumers to lend in all ways including via credit cards.

- **Expired Card** - An expired card is one with an encoded or printed date on it that make it unusable after stated date. The date of expiration varies depending on the policy of the card company.

- **Fair Credit Billing Act** - The purpose of the Fair Credit Billing Act is to protect credit card owners from unfair billing and to give a mechanism of appeal for said errors. Examples of the errors would be: charges of the wrong amount, charges not actually made by the consumer, items not received by the customer, charges for damaged goods on delivery, statement mailed to the wrong address etc. A consumer is able to dispute a particular charge by mailing his or her name to the address on their credit card statement that says "billing inquiries". The dispute must be made within 60 days. The credit issuer should acknowledge the dispute within 30 days, and within 90 days make the correction if needed.

- **Fair Credit Reporting Act** - The Fair Credit Reporting Act, which was a 2003 amendment, allows customers the privilege to receive free copies of their credit reports each year from the three major credit bureaus. The Act regulates how credit bureaus correct, maintain, and share information on the credit reports. It sets a base of consumer credit right, and allows consumers the right to have inaccurate information removed from the files.

- **Fair Isaac** - A Fair Isaac is first name FICO was known for. The company provides credit scores along with decision making services and is intended to help financial services companies. The Fair Isaac changed its name to FICO in 2009.

- **FAKO score** - A FAKO score is used to describe a score that is not associated with a FICO credit score. If a consumer purchases his or her score from anywhere but myfico.com the score would be considered a FAKO score instead of a FICO score.

- **Federal Deposit Insurance Corporation** - The FDIC is a federal agency that was created by Congress to assure a consumer that deposits will be made, and that a consumer has protection for his or her money, and that financial institutions are stable. It requires banks to have a certain amount of capital available at all times and insures its depositors that they will be insured up to $250,000.

- **Federal funds rate** - The federal funds rate is an interest rate that banks will lend balances capital, usually overnight, to other depository institutions. The rate of interest is decided between the two banks and is the weighted average through all transactions. It is important to to credit card holders with different credit rates. The federal funds rate is three points higher than the prime rate (the credit rate that is charged by banks to their customers; it is usually the same through major banks) and usually changes in direct correlation to the prime rate.

- **Federal Trade Commission** - The Federal Trade Commission is in promotes fair and free trade for the consumer. It prevents price-fixing agreements, false advertising, illegal combinations of competitors etc.

- **FICO** - FICO was founded in 1956, it is a type of credit score. It is a three digit value that shows the risk of a credit borrower. A consumer's score ranges from 300 to 850; the higher the score, the better. Usually, a person with a low FICO score can expect to have higher interest rates on loans.

- **Finance Charge** - A finance charge is a fee associated with the cost of borrowing. It includes the cost of interest and additional fees. The charge will be a numerical dollar value.

- **Fixed Rate** - A fixed rate APR is a per-unit cost that does not change throughout the year. It is a predetermined rate that is set for a certain amount of time.

- **Fleet Cards** - Fleet cards are usually associated with businesses and are used most commonly for auto expenses such as maintenance and gas.

- **Floor Limit** - A floor limit is a certain amount that MasterCard and Visa has determined for which credit and debit transaction for single transactions must amount to at merchant outlets and branches.

- **Foreign Transaction Fee** - A foreign transaction fee is a charge that many credit card companies, such as Visa and MasterCard, put on cards when purchases are made in countries that do not have a dollar currency or involve a foreign bank. The fee is usually a percentage of the purchase. It is also called a foreign exchange fee or currency conversion fee.

- **Fraud Alert** - A fraud alert helps protect your credit card information. It is an alert on your credit card account or a credit bureau that is placed by the owner or the issuer of the card. If questionable actions are made regarding the account, it is flagged for a security check.

- **Fraudulent Transaction** - A fraudulent transaction is one that is not made by the card holder. These transactions will be listed in different ways depending on the card company.

- **Fraudulent User** - A fraudulent user is someone who uses credit card information from another person without authorization. They will use the information to purchase goods or services unbeknownst to the credit cardholder.

- **Go-To Rate** - A go-to rate is an interest rate put on credit cards after the beginning period, sometime known as the teaser period.

- **Grace Period** - A grace period is the time, usually a month or more, before a debtor will have dues be paid with interest. A typical grace period is 31 days. According to Credit CARD Act of 2009, grace periods must be at least 21 days. It usually only applies to new purchases.

- **Gross Pay** - A persons gross pay is the total allowances, commissions, overtime pay, bonuses, etc. before there are any deductions like taxes.

- **Guarantor** - A guarantor is also known as co-signer would be someone who agrees to pay the loan of another person if he or she defaults on the obligation. It often times makes a lender more willing to approve a particular loan for a borrower of high-risk.

- **Hard Inquiry** - A hard inquiry is an indication on an individual's credit score that someone has asked for a copy. They are the result of an individual who applies for a loan or a mortgage. The hard inquiry has a minuscule negative impact on a person's credit score.

- **Hold** - A hold occurs for example when a person checks into a hotel or rents a car and the issuer will charge an estimated amount until the final amount is determined. The final amount can be released within minutes or hours or even days.

- **Identity Theft** - Identity theft refers to fraud that involves the use of another person's personal information such as their name, Social Security number, credit card number etc. without the individuals knowledge.

- **Inactive Account** - An inactive account is a bank account on which no transaction has occurred within a certain amount of time. If too long of a time has passed, in the case of credit card accounts, some card issuers can opt to close the account and take away charging privileges.

- **Inactivity Fee** - An inactivity fee is imposed by certain banks on a credit card account that is not used for a certain amount of time. It is a way banks were able to increase their income in 2009 and 2010 but the Credit CARD Act has banned inactivity fees now.

- **Interchange Fee** - An interchange fee is a term used to describe a fee paid by a business owners bank to a customer's bank when merchants accept credit cards as a form of payment. The amount varies, but it is usually around 2 percent of the total. The fee for purchases that are made in person are usually cheaper than those that are made online because the card is present and can be inspected.

- **Interest Rate** - An interest rate is the price a borrower must pay for taking out a loan. An interest rate may be more complicated in the case of a credit card account due to the fact that lenders will add different types of interest rates. The beginning rate will be low, but new rates can be added with additional purchases.

- **Interest Rate Cap** - An interest rate cap is a limit on how high an interest rate can be set for a customer. They can be obligatory in a credit card agreement or by law.

- **Introductory Period** - An introductory period is a certain amount of time in which a certain percentage rate stays the same. Wants the amount of time is up, the rate will usually go up.

- **Introductory Rate** - The introductory annual percentage rate is a temporary lower annual rate that is offered by credit card companies to interest a customer in applying for that particular card. The rate does not usually stay the same after the first year, but according to the Credit CARD Act of 2009 the Introductory Rate must last at a minimum of six months.

- **Issuer** - An issuer is a corporation that issues credit cards. A credit card issuer is not MasterCard or Visa, they are transaction processors.

- **Joint Account** - A joint account is a bank account that is owned by two or more people. Each person involved has withdrawal and deposit privileges; also, if something goes wrong with the account such as fraud, defaults or overdrafts all parties will be held accountable.

- **Keep and Pay** - Keep and pay is a tactic that makes it possible for an individual who declares bankruptcy to maintain ownership of certain assets. You are able to avoid going to court, but since the debt is not on court documents, the individual is able to continue paying for the purchased item as agreed originally.

- **Late Payment Fee** - A late payment fee is a charge that is imposed on an individual for not paying his or her debt on time. It is possible that late payments can negatively affect your credit history.

- **Libor** - Libor is also is short for the London Interbank Offered Rate. It is a daily reference rate that is based on the interest rates that banks use to lend money back and forth in the London wholesale market.

- **Line of Credit** - A line of credit can take many forms: cash, credit, overdraft, term loan, discounting or purchase of commercial bills etc. It is a way for an individual to borrow and access money up to a certain limit and pay the money back and then be able to borrow again. A person's line of credit can be secured or unsecured and the interest rates are usually variable depending on the line.

- **Loyalty Programs** - A loyalty program is a structured effort to encourage credit card customers to use specific cards. They are generally called rewards cards, discount cards, or point cards. For example, an airline company may offer airline miles that counts towards the cheaper purchase of a ticket by using their card.

- **Magnetic Stripe** - A magnetic strip connects you with the credit or debit card and your account number. The card will work when connected with a device that reads the information on the magnetic strip. It is separated into three parts: the first and second part is used to hold the information about your credit account and any other information is stored on the third part.

- **Margin** - The margin is the difference between the variable interest rate and the prime interest rate. When an issuer sends out a monthly statement or opens an account for someone, that information for the variable interest rate must be shown.

- **Merchant Agreement** - A merchant agreement is a written contract between a bank and a merchant that details the terms and conditions related to the use of bank cards and anything related to its activity.

- **Merchant Bank** - A merchant bank is a credit card processing bank that has an agreement for a particular merchant to receive credit for deposits from bank card transactions minus a processing fee.

- **Minimum Finance Charge** - A minimum finance charge is the smallest amount that must be paid on the balance of a credit card bill from the previous billing cycle. The charge is usually around $0.50 which can be higher than the finance charge. A minimum finance charge is different than a minimum payment.

- **Minimum Payment** - A minimum payment is the smallest amount of money that a borrower must pay on a credit card statement for the month. Each credit card company can have different amount that will be due, but the "terms and conditions" document will outline the requirements for how much must be paid. Recently, the minimum payment has been raised from around the 2% it was because borrowers were long periods of time to pay off debts.

- **Money Market** - The money market rate is used as an average rate for interest on bank funds. Two of the most common referred to are U.S. Treasury notes and LIBOR (London Interbank Offered Rate).

- **Monthly Periodic Rate** - A monthly periodic rate is a rate and balance calculation method used for computing an individual's credit card bill. Once this is found, it will be multiplied the balance on the credit card to figure out the interest rate on a monthly basis.

- **Monthly Statement** - A monthly statement is a statement that is mailed or found online by the bank for each account that shows all credit card transactions during a particular month. It shows any activity by the consumer such as payments, purchases or any charge put on the card.

- **National Bank** - A national bank is a commercial bank that is chartered by the federal government. It is supervised by the OCC (Office of the Comptroller of the Currency) and is required to be a part of the Federal deposit Insurance Corporation. Most credit card companies are part of a national bank.

- **National Issuers** - When a bank issues credit cards all over the United States, it is called a national issuer. Unlike a state or regional issuer, a national issuer lender is friendly in all fifty states.

- **Negative Information** - Negative Information is information that appears on a credit report that will negatively affect an individual when applying for a loan. The information can stay on record for as long as ten years depending on the type of information.

- **Net Pay** - Net Pay is the money left over after the deductions from gross salary are made like taxes.
- **New Balance** - The new balance is what is still owed on a credit card bill. It shows charges and payments from the last month and recent purchases along with other fees.
- **NFC** - NFC stands for near field communication which means that there is a way for data technology to transfer from one wireless portal to another as long as they are a short distance away. For example your cell phone would be considered a NFC and would be able to communicate with some sort of remote computer to accept the message sent.
- **Office of Comptroller of the Currency (OCC)** - The Office of the Comptroller and the Currency (OCC) is a federal agency that is in charge of supervising of federal branches and agencies in the United States that issue credit cards.
- **Online Bill Presentment and Payment** - By using online bill presentation and payment a customer is able to view and pay his or her bill online by transferring money from his/her checking account. There is no paper used when using online bill presentation and payment.
- **Open End** - An open end loan is a loan where the total amount can be changed without re-negotiating the terms on the loan. The change can be good or bad depending on the risk there is in the eyes of the lender.
- **Opt Out** - Opt out is an option that consumers have when the interest rates on a debt owed increases or if there are changes in the terms predetermined. There must be forty five days advanced notice before changes are made so that the consumer is able to choose whether or not to opt out. A consumer must pay his or her debt within five years though if they use the opt-out option.
- **Over-Limit** - When a consumer is over his/her limit it means that he/she has attempted to make a charge to an account that does

not have sufficient funds. The card issuer might decline the transaction or their will be a fee for over-limit.

- **Over-Limit Fee** - An over-limit fee is associated with a transaction that is made to an account with insufficient funds. The fee is usually very large but under the Credit CARD Act of 2009, an issuer must give the consumer the option of choosing between a declined purchase or a fee for allowing the transaction when setting up an account.

- **Overdraft Protection** - When an individual attempts to withdraw more money than is available in a particular account (a checking account, savings account or any other line of credit), overdraft protection automatically transfers funds from one account into another to prevent overdraft fees. Overdraft protection, though, has fees and an individual can chose whether he or she wants this insurance.

- **Payment Due Date** - A payment due date is the particular date that a minimum payment is required to be paid by for an account every month.

- **Payment History** - When an individual is applying for a loan with good rates, he/she wants a good payment history of on-time payments and good credit. A payment history shows an individual's credit rate over time.

- **Penalty Rate** - A penalty rate is triggered by a consumer making late payments. It is usually several points higher than the current interest rate and it is charged by the credit card issuer.

- **Per Transaction Fees** - A per transaction fee is associated with a merchants account. It means that every time a customer uses a credit/debit card for a transaction there is a fee to the merchant that is associated with that charge.

- **Periodic Statement** - A periodic statement, also known as a billing statement or a monthly statement, is a record that is drawn up about once a month to show a consumer all of his/her transactions during that time. It includes payment, fees, charges, and purchases and is available by mail or electronically.

- **PIN (personal identification number)** - A personal identification number is associated with a debit card that is like a password for a transaction to be accepted. It is a series of numbers that a card holder chooses when setting up his/her account. It also works to use a signature instead of putting in a pin number when making a transaction.

- **PIN cashing** - PIN cashing is fraud that allows an individual to withdraw cash from a victims credit line by using stolen debit/credit card information.

- **Point of Sale Terminal** - A point of sale terminal in terms of a credit card is the machine that the card can be swiped through and how the merchant is able to record receiving the payment. The transaction begins when the card is swiped and is completed when the payment is approved.

- **POS (Point of Sale)** - The point of sale or the checkout is the place where the transaction occurs. There is an exchange between a merchant and a customer: goods or services are exchanged for payment.

- **Post Date** - The Post Date is the day when a credit card company will become aware and place on their books a purchase made by a credit card owner.

- **Preapproval** - Preapproval is something done by credit card issuers. They can see an individual's credit score and decide that he or she is eligible for a credit card by that particular company. An individual cannot be solicited to until he or she is over the age of 21. It is also known as prescreening.

- **Preapproved** - An individual who has been preapproved means that he or she has been screened for their credit score and deemed eligible for a credit card by a particular credit card company because his or her score is high enough. If an individual agrees the credit card issuers will decide on a annual rate percentage based on the individuals current credit score.

- **Prepaid Cards** - A prepaid card is a card that works when purchasing items. There is a certain amount of money deposited onto the card at an earlier time and can be used until it reaches the amount deposited. They work like store-value cards.

- **Prime Borrower** - A prime borrower is an individual with excellent credit scores and is acknowledged for paying off their debts on time. They are usually offered significantly lower interest rates due to their previous history.
- **Prime Credit** - A prime credit means that an individual has a notable credit record and is acknowledged for paying debts on time. Individuals with prime credit are offered exceptional terms when being given credit. There is no defining score that separates individuals from having non-prime credit and usually varies from company to company.
- **Prime Rate** - Also referred to as prime lending rate, this is the referenced interest rate used by banks as the annual percentage rate to quote loans against.
- **Prime Rate (or prime interest rate)** - A prime rate is a rate that is 3% higher than the rate set by a bank. Most banks tend to have similar rates. Wall Street Journal is known for comparing the prime rates of different banks.
- **Purchase Rate** - A purchase rate is a particular interest rate that an individual would be charged for purchasing something with his or her credit card. The rate is usually significantly lower than the rate that would be made for borrowing money because a credit card issuer or a bank would consider a daily purchase as something that is not as risky as lending money in advance.
- **Qualifying Ratio** - A qualifying ratio is a ratio that compares an individual's monthly obligations (other debts such as student loans, car payments etc.) to the individuals monthly gross income. Depending on the particular lender, the ratio that is considered acceptable varies depending on the particular company.
- **Reloadable** - A reloadable card is a prepaid card that can have money added to it after the purchase date. There is usually a charge for issuing the card and then for adding money too it.
- **Remote Deposit Capture (RDC)** - Depositing a check through a mobile device, like a smartphone or tablet. Pictures taken with the device are used to identify key information on checks, which is then verified by a bank or third party organization.

- **Returned Payment Fee** - A returned payment fee is a fee associated with bill paid by a bounced check. The individual who writes the bounced check will have to pay a fee.

- **Revolving Balance** - Revolving balance is debt that is still owed on a credit card after a billing cycle. The amount changes by cycle depending on how much an individual pays off or how much is added to the debt. Once a debt is paid off the revolving balance is no longer there.

- **Reward Card** - A reward card is credit card that offers benefits based upon the card's usage. The rewards vary but usually consist of airline tickets, discounts on future purchases, or cash refunds.

- **Risk-Based Pricing** - Risk-based pricing is a form of interest rate that is decided by an individual's credit score and history of repayment. It is different for everyone.

- **Secured Credit Cards** - A secured credit card is a credit card that targets individuals with no credit history or poor credit history. They usually have high fees attached to them because individuals purchasing them do not have many other options. They also usually also require some sort of deposit before they are issued.

- **Security Code** - A security code are digits that are associated with a credit card to verify the ownership of the card. The security code is usually three or four numbers long and can be on the front or the back of the card. Each credit card company usually has a different name for the security code such as a "card verification code"

- **Standard APR** - A standard APR is something that begins after the introductory period has ended. The APR will come in many forms and each is associated with different actions made by a credit card owner such as a purchase or a balance transfer.

- **Statement** - A statement is a record of every transaction that occurred during a billing cycle. It is prepared by a financial institution and includes anything from a withdrawal of money to interest earned.

- **Stored-Value Card** - A stored-value card is a device that has a computer chip recorded with a certain amount of money. It is about the size of a credit card. If it is re-loadable then it is re-usable and money can be added to it from a teller machine.

- **Subprime Credit Card** - A subprime credit card is a credit card that is geared towards individuals who do not have a prime credit history. They usually have high charges associated with them because the issuer is at a higher risk of an individual defaulting on payments.

- **Tabling** - Tabling occurs when credit card companies advertise to students on college campuses to encourage them to sign up credit cards by offering gifts. Usually there will be tables set up by the card issuer in locations that are highly populated by college students.

- **Teaser Rate** - A teaser rate is an interest rate put on credit cards at the beginning period. It lasts at least six months and then will usually rise significantly. It is sometimes known as the go-to rate.

- **Terms and Conditions** - The terms and conditions of an agreement between a credit card issuer and a credit card company describe the rules and regulations that the credit card issuer goes by. Once the card is used for the first time, the terms and conditions of the credit card become legally binding.

- **Tiered Rewards** - Tiered rewards are rewards that give a certain percentage of money back. As the amount of spending on the account increases, the percentage back increases as well. When someone spends $1000 they might get .25% back, and for each additional amount of money a higher they will receive a higher increment of a percentage back.

- **Total Finance Charge** - The total finance charge is the total amount of money that a consumer pays that he/she borrows with a credit card. It would be the amount borrowed plus interest.

- **Truth in Lending Act** - The Truth in Lending act promotes having credit card owners becoming more informed when deciding which card to use. It gives consumers more accurate information so they are able to compare different credit cards before choosing. Credit card issuers are required to give all information about the terms and conditions of the credit card so that consumers are not misinformed.

- **Truth in Savings Act** - The Truth in Savings Act is a law that requires any bank or other type of association to put forth information about charges on deposit accounts that have to do with interest rates or any other charge. It commonly is referred to as the FDIC Improvement Act or Regulation DD.
- **Two-Cycle Billing** - Two-cycle billing a way to calculate how much interest must be paid on balances left on credit cards from month to month. It considers the current balance on the credit card and the average daily balance from the previous billing period. It was banned by the Credit CARD Act of 2009. It is also known as double-cycle billing.
- **Universal Default** - Universal default makes it possible for credit card issuers to raise interest rates for a change in the lenders profile. For example, if a credit card holder does not make his or her payments on time then a credit card issuer has the option to raise the interest rate.
- **Unsecured Credit Cards** - An unsecured credit card does not require a security deposit to place a limit on the card. It is also not secured by collateral meaning it is not connected to the customer's property making it impossible for the lender to seize it. The lender must come up with other means of receiving payment if a customer defaults on his or her payment.
- **User Authentication** - User authentication is the process by which a system verifies the identity of an individual attempting to access it. It verifies the credit card holder's identity.
- **Utilization Ratio** - The utilization ratio is important in determining ones credit score. It will compare the amount of credit an individual is using with how much is available to the customer. It is better for an individual to have a low utilization ratio because that means that there is lower debt obligation and more available credit.
- **Variable Interest Rate** - A variable interest rate is an interest rate that fluctuates over time. These rates are pegged to prime rates. The prime rate is determined by the Federal Reserve and the variable interest rate will follow the prime rate when it fluctuates. Your variable interest rate will be the prime rate plus a certain amount.

- **Visa** - Visa is a processor of transactions, either debit or credit, through its payments network. It has more than 13,300 institutions and about 520 million cards that it provides to customers.
- **Visa Issuer** - A visa issuer is responsible for issuing a credit or debit card to an individual.
- **Void** - A void is a way to terminate a transaction and nullify it. It will no longer be settled and will be removed.
- **Wall Street Journal Prime Rate** - A common way to determine the prime rate. It is an index that is 3 percent higher than the federal funds rate. The Wall Street Journal takes a survey of thirty of the largest banks and assesses their prime rates. These rates are published in their print edition.
- **X (Regulation X)** - Regulation X a rule set by the Federal Reserve Board that puts a limit on the amount of credit that is allowed of financial institutions.
- **Yield on Earning Assets** - Yield on earning assets is a way to determine the solvency of a financial industry that is used by banking regulators. It is a percentage of average earning assets that comes from interest, dividend or income earned from loans or investments.
- **Z Score** - The z-score looks at how likely it is that a bank will become bankrupt. It is a formula that puts a value on five financial ratios. It was determined by Professor Edward Altman at the New York University in 1968.
- **Zero Balance** - Zero balance means that an individual has no debt on his or her credit card. By leaving a credit card at zero balance there is a possibility of losing some credit history and could potentially hurt your credit score, but might be negligible if you continue making payments on time and using the credit card smartly.

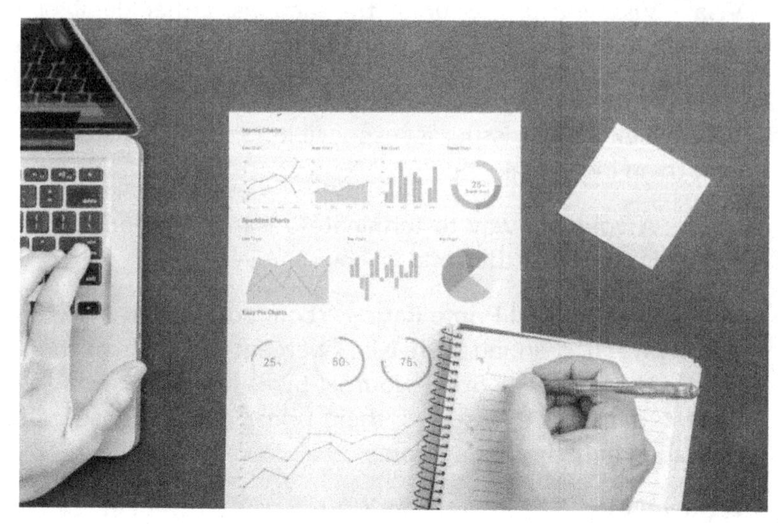

SAMPLE CREDIT REPAIR BONUS LETTERS

Sample Credit Repair Letter

Current Date

Full Name
Street Address
City, State and zip code
SSN:
Date of Birth:

Credit Bureau Name:
Credit Bureau Address:
Credit Bureau City, State and Zip

RE: Complaint Letter to Investigate and Delete Inaccurate Information

Dear Sir or Madam:

I respectfully request your prompt attention on the following inaccurate information on my credit report. For your convenience, the disputed item is listed on the enclosed page of my credit report.

The following item is inaccurate and negatively effecting my credit. Please reinvestigate this matter and delete and/or correct the disputed item. I respectfully request that you provide me with proof of the disputed item, specifically any contract, note, court documents or any instrument bearing my signature. Failing that, this item must be deleted.

Item: {Account Name}
Account # {Account Number}
Dispute Reason: {This account is not reporting correctly, this account was a Paid Collection, Ect.}
Dispute Instruction: {Please investigate and delete this account}

It is my understanding that under law you have 30 days from the receipt of this letter to verify this item. It should be understood that failure to do so within the 30 day period constitutes reason to immediately delete this item from my credit report. {FCRA 15 U.SC. section 1681 (5) (A).

Also, pursuant to 15 U.S.C. section 1681i (6) (A) of the Fair Credit Reporting Act, please notify me the item has been deleted. You may send an updated copy of my credit report to the below address. According to the provisions of 15 U.S.C. section 1681j, there should be no charge for this notification.

Sincerely,
Your Name

Sample Collection Company Request for Validation not Verification

Current Date

Full Name
Street Address
City, State and zip code

Collection Company Name:
Collection Company Address:
Collection Company, State and Zip

RE : Collection Account Name   Collection Account #

To Whom It May Concern:

This letter is being sent to you in response to notices sent to me from your company and more importantly, due to your erroneous reporting to the Credit Bureau{s}, the highly negative impact on my personal credit report. Please be advised that this is not a refusal to pay, but a notice sent pursuant to the Fair Debt Collection Practices Act, 15 USC 1692g Sec. 809 {b} that your claim is disputed and validation is requested.

This is NOT a request for "verification" or proof of my mailing address, but a request for VALIDATION made pursuant to the above named Title and Section. I respectfully request that your offices provide me with competent evidence that I have any legal obligation to pay you.

Please provide me with the following:

- What the money you say I owe is for:
- Explain and show me how you calculated what you say I owe:

- Provide me with copies of any papers that show I agreed to pay what you say I owe:
- Provide a verification or copy of any judgment if applicable:
- Identify the original creditor:
- Prove the Statute of Limitations has not expired on this account:
- Show me the you are licensed to collect in my state:
- Provide me with your license numbers and Registered Agent or Agent of Service:

At this time I will also inform you that if your offices have reported invalidated information to any of the 3 major Credit Bureau's {Experian, Equifax or TransUnion} this action might constitute fraud under both Federal and State Laws. Due to this fact, if any negative mark is found on any of my credit reports by your company or the company that you represent, I will not hesitate to bring legal action against you for the following:

- Violation of the Fair Credit Reporting Act
- Violation of the Fair Debt Collection Practices Act
- Defamation of Character

If your offices are able to provide proper documentation as requested in the following Declaration, I will require at least 30 days to investigate this information and during such time all collection activity must cease and desist.

Also, during this validation period, if any action is taken which could be considered detrimental to any of my credit reports, I will consult with my legal counsel for suit. This includes listing any information with a credit reporting repository that could be inaccurate or invalidated or verifying an account as accurate, when it fact there is no provided proof that it is accurate.

If your company fails to respond to this validation request within 30 days from the date of your receipt, all references to this account must be deleted and completely removed from my credit report and a copy of such deletion {to any/all of the 3 major credit reporting bureaus: Equifax, Experian and TransUnion} request shall be sent to me immediately.

I would also like to request, in writing, that no telephone contact be made by your company to my home or my place of employment. If your offices attempt telephone communication with me, including but not limited to computer generated calls and calls or correspondence sent to or with any third parties, it will be considered harassment and I will have no choice but to file suit. All future communications with me MUST be done in writing and sent to the address noted in this letter by USPS.

It would be advisable that you assure your records are in order before I am forced to take legal action against your company and your client. This is an attempt to correct your records; any information obtained shall be used for that purpose.

Sincerely,

Your Name

Sample to Investigate and Remove Unauthorized Inquiries

Current Date

Full Name
Street Address
City, State and zip code
SSN:
Date of Birth:

Credit Bureau Name:
Credit Bureau Address:
Credit Bureau City, State and Zip
Re: Complaint Letter to Investigate and Delete Inaccurate Information

Dear Sir or Madam:
I am writing to you to request that you remove the following unauthorized inquiry(ies) from my credit report:

Creditor: {Creditor Name}
Inquiry Date: {List Inquiry Date}
Attached is a copy of the letter that I have sent directly to the creditor disputing their reporting.
I understand that per the Fair Credit Reporting Act, you are required to notify me of your investigation results within 30 days. My contact information is provided below and I have included proof of my social security and current address to avoid any delays in your response time.
I look forward to receiving an updated copy of my credit report reflecting the above correction. Thanking you in advance.
Sincerely,

Your Name

Resources

My Fico, About Credit Scores
http://www.myfico.com/crediteducation/creditscores.aspx

What Is a Good Credit Score?
https://www.credit.com/credit-scores/what-is-a-good-credit-score/

Money Under 30, Understanding "Your Number"
http://www.moneyunder30.com/what-is-a-credit-score

Bankrate, Credit Scores Explained
http://www.bankrate.com/brm/news/cc/20010223a.asp

U.S. General Services Administration, Federal Citizen Information Center and Fair Isaac Corporation (2008)
http://publications.usa.gov/USAPubs.php?PubID=3379

Federal Trade Commission's, Facts for Consumers (2011)
http://www.ftc.gov/bcp/edu/pubs/consumer/credit/cre34.shtm

Federal Trade Commisson's Fair Credit Reporting Act
https://www.ftc.gov/enforcement/rules/rulemaking-regulatory-reform-proceedings/fair-credit-reporting-act

Fair Debt Collection Practices Act
https://www.ftc.gov/enforcement/rules/rulemaking-regulatory-reform-proceedings/fair-debt-collection-practices-act-text

United States Courts's - Process - Bankruptcy Basics
https://www.uscourts.gov/services-forms/bankruptcy/bankruptcy-basics/process-bankruptcy-basics

TransUnion
https://www.transunion.com/

Experian
https://www.experian.com/blogs/ask-experian/

Equifax
https://www.equifax.com/personal/education/credit/report/

About The Author

President and Owner of *Credit360 Credit Repair*, Andre Coakley, was raised in Miami, Florida, in a single parent household with his mother. While growing up as on only child, he spent much of his time alone while his mother pursued her PhD in Early Childhood Development. Though he had times of loneliness, seeing his mother's determination to earn her doctorate and his father's tireless work ethic in overcoming poverty, inspired and stuck with Andre as he grew into an adult.

Upon graduating from high school, he attended *Bethune-Cookman University* where he earned a Bachelor's of Science degree. Not long after, he opened *Absolute Mortgage & Investments Corp* as their President and Principle broker. Although his role as a Principal Mortgage Broker allowed him financial freedom, however the economic downturn of the 2008 recession led to the foreclosure of his home and the eventual closing of his mortgage company. Even while having the proper knowledge of credit and finances, he wasn't able to avoid this economic downfall. After getting back on his feet, Andre realized that his professional skills were best used in the credit industry. Wanting to help others repair their credit, he transitioned to the field of credit and finance. Since making this transition, he has successfully completed training in programs such as *FDIC* Money Smart Train the Trainer, Housing Counseling, Pre-Purchase Home ownership Education, Credit Counseling for Maximum Results, and many others. Andre has also earned the designation of an *FICO* Certified Credit Specialist and an Ambassador Instructor of the *Credit Repair University*.

Now equipped with over 20 plus years of extensive financial knowledge, he has since then, served as the Founder, Director and CEO of his own 501©3 Non-profit Organization, *Community Works Coalitions Inc*. Along with this, and his role in *Credit360 Credit Repair*, Andre is also the founder of the *7-Figure Start-up Academy* a business mentoring firm that has coached over 300 companies to date.

As someone who has struggled with hardships and poor credit, he knows first-hand just how difficult circumstances can become. Not wanting others to experience the same, Andre uses his experience and in depth knowledge to help individuals, families and businesses learn the strategies needed to repair and rebuild their credit. With the right education, others can avoid the pitfalls Andre once faced, and most importantly, be prepared for the unexpected.

His work in this area has allowed him numerous awards including the *Millionaires Club Award* which recognized him for earning over $1,000,000 while using *Credit Repair Cloud Software*. These and Andre's other achievements have also allowed him to proudly serve as a member on the *Miami Dade Advocacy Trust - Economic Development Advocacy Trust Committee*. Away from this and his career in credit and finance, Andre enjoys traveling to different countries abroad and taking 24 mile bike rides. More than anything, however, he loves spending his free time with his sons, Amari and Kameron.

Made in United States
North Haven, CT
01 July 2024